WAR BABY

❧

A Memoir of the Path of Dark and Light

By Dougald Blue III

WAR BABY

is a work of non-fiction.
The events presented are true; however,
names and identities of many
of the people mentioned
have been altered to protect privacy
and maintain anonymity.

The author's contact information can be
found at the end of the book.

The cover photograph was
composed and captured by the author,
Dougald L. Blue III.

The book was designed by
Lucy Alfriend Thacker.

ISBN 13:978-1490334677

CONTENTS

DEDICATION

For those who seek

PROLOGUE

"When I had journeyed half of our life's way,
I found myself within a shadowed forest,
for I had lost the path that does not stray."

The Divine Comedy of Dante Alighieri
Inferno: Canto I, 1

Translation by Allen Mandelbaum,
Everyman's Library
(New York, Alfred A. Knopf, a division of Random House, 1995), page 59.

PART ONE

Mind-Reading, and Other Things
Southerners Don't Talk About

CHAPTER ONE

THE NINE-MILLIMETER GERMAN LUGER– a rare, long-barreled naval officer's version– was kept in the same spot in the same drawer of the same dresser for the last thirty years, ready for use. The hand-made hardwood dresser was one of a matched pair in my parents' room in the home I had grown up in and where I was now alone.

I knew how to handle the Luger. I could fire it, take it apart, clean it, and put it back together. I recalled where I had kept some bullets. And a magazine to hold them. I went there, to my old room, my old dresser still in place. So were the bullets.

Opening the box, I took out a nine-millimeter Luger round. I liked the feel of its solidity in my fingers, its appearance that of a miniature ICBM, its blunt tip, one that would open and spread upon impact, causing maximum trauma.

I liked that, too– maximum trauma. I knew what it looked like. Once in younger happier days, I had taken the Luger to the area on the farm where it was safe to shoot targets. I had a watermelon. I disliked watermelons because they were so messy. I was about to see how much messier they could get.

I propped the melon on a leaning worn wooden fence post next to a little pond with a wild-flowered berm behind it. There were no houses out in that direction. Just woods, shielded by the berm.

I walked back about 25 yards. To chamber a round, you pulled back the receiver and let it close. With a satisfying metallic clack a bullet was in place, ready to be fired. I flicked the safety off, took careful aim with my dominant right eye. One always kept both eyes open upon aiming. My dad, and the U.S. Army, had taught me how to fire accurately, and that was the key.

The forward sight lined up perfectly on the heart of the watermelon, now nestled in the rear sight's aperture. I took a couple of deep breaths, then a third, held it lightly at mid-breath and squeezed the trigger. The satisfying report, kickback, and flare from the barrel preceded by an instant the explosion of the melon into a cloud of red and green.

My father had always kept the Luger in good working order, ready to use. More fire-power was in the house too. Rifles were in the corner behind the closet door. One was mine, the other my dad's. I had grown up in that Southern tradition of maintaining arms– a holdover from earlier times, times shrouded in tradition and history. But at the moment, the Luger in the other room was on my mind, its longtime curated presence perversely calming, for this was fast becoming the worst day of my life.

I had been found out. My carefully cultivated cover was blown– and all by a simple phone call for help to a psychiatrist– one I thought of as a family friend to whom I had reached out for help.

As I look back on it, his brusque, frank, confrontive response to my cry for help was exactly correct. But at the time I was shocked, angry, and scared. Details of the guns snaked through my mind as I faced what I might do.

Standing there in my old room, suicide and murder joined foggy confusion and relentless depression. Once more I fingered a round from my box. In just milliseconds the dark vortex in my mind suffocated any rational thought I might have clung to. Knowing it just takes one, I pulled three of the rounds from the box in my drawer anyway. I inserted them in the top of my magazine, pushing each downward against the spring inside.

I thought not of what I might do next, as what had just happened to me confounded any scheme I might have had straightening myself out. A drink would have helped. Several in fact. But the house had been left bereft of alcohol. Someone's premonition?

A sepulchral voice deep within seemed to say, "it was alcohol that got you to this place."

I had begun to drink regularly when I left home to go to college because "a glass of the finest" greased the wheels of academia, and that was what one needed to do.

The classical Georgian symmetry of the fraternity house was all lit up, all three floors. I had finished three days of x-ing tiny boxes, blacking-in wee oblongs— "freshman orientation," they called it. They were trying to psychoanalyze me with a whirlwind of paper, all of which would go into a big machine that read the number-two-pencil x's and oblongs and predict what I was going to be when I grew up. And what classes I ought to take, my aptitudes and abilities. Maybe what kind of student I would be, too.

I could have saved them the trouble. My next move was laden with prophecy. I needed to get to the real deal, and the first step of fraternity rush was on. So I was glad to get away from the testing, for fraternity circle was alive and waiting to introduce innocents like me to its Nineteenth Century brotherhoods... and another kind of testing.

My roommate and I stepped onto the white-columned portico, where "brothers" waited to greet us. One thrust a milkshake cup full of beer into my hand. Bo Diddley riffed and wailed from the sound system inside. The tone was raucous. The large living room was packed with guys— each of us between 18 and 22 or so— all seeming to talk at the same time. Some kind of code was being exchanged. "Where you from?" "Where'd you go to school?"– that kind of thing, with jollity all around, hale-fellows, well-met, bound for glorious futures. But beneath it all, the real question was "Who's your daddy?"

So, yeah, this was where I needed to be. After the third milkshake cup of beer I decided I had pretty much arrived. The college scene of the 60s, a place and time now frozen in memory, was an era still fueled by earlier times. The portrait of Robert E. Lee on the wall told that story. I recently heard a celebrated journalist and historian liken his alma mater– a similar Southern institution– to a mélange of *Brideshead Revisited* and *Deliverance*. The metaphor would have fit perfectly that day all those years ago.

On the way back to my dorm that night, I threw up three times, once on the well-tended rosebushes of the head of the English department, a bad portent capping the start of an even worse pattern, one that would last a long time.

The thought of becoming alcoholic never entered my mind. In fact I had no idea what alcoholism was. If I considered it at all, I figured chronic drinking just happened to bums and street people. How did street people get there? I would learn how.

But then, when I thought that way, the sun nevertheless always seemed to shine in those days. We had other, more sophisticated dysfunctions in my family. Seeing a psychiatrist, for example, was some sort of rite of passage in our circles. Being Southerners, however, we did not speak of it, except in hushed tones and very rarely. It was right up there with Religion, Money and Politics– "things," my patrician grandmother taught me, "we don't discuss in polite society."

The danger in her advice, of course, led to that peculiar Southern way in which what you saw was not what you got. So when the tones were hushed and moods somber, I learned to listen up. What I heard was likely to be about somebody having a "nervous breakdown" or "depression." I overheard the old ladies speak in lowered octaves that you just knew as a kid you had to hear– especially when they mentioned "going to Duke."

"Going-to-Duke" meant psychiatric care at the university's medical center.

And in a respectable North Carolina family, Duke was the place to go when you went 'round the bend.

But in the panoply of hidden whackeries, it seemed to me that depression was borderline fashionable. There were news items and movies with a patina of the illuminati about them when it came to depression. I learned a lot about that waiting in endless lines at the A&P, reading the tabloids.

Same with the "nervous breakdown"– still spoken of sotto voce– but more and more looking to me like something almost okay, maybe some sort of secret handshake among the New South's cognoscenti.

So how about me? Would I get my turn?

Of course. Depression would become my delusional self-talk for any ideas about "problem drinking" I might have. It became a safe harbor because it was deal-with-able. I could look it up in books and spout pseudo-scholarly patter about the new cross I bore– the one that explained certain things. Little did I know that this mental construct was a cover-up, an excuse. Years later I would hear the counselors call it "denial."

The depression ruse was not needed right away, because for the first few years, I was in college and any occasional problem where alcohol was in play was excusable as "just boys being boys," and "you work hard, you play hard." Such excuses blocked connecting the dots. That would take a long time.

Snickers twittered through the assembly in the college's auditorium, as the dean of students, dressed in a conservative tweed jacket, button-down white shirt and a maroon-and-gray striped tie, concluded his opening remarks to the incoming class this way: "Remember this, gentlemen, the ax falls in the sophomore year. Look at the man on your left. Look at the man on your right. Probability tells us they will not be there when you graduate in four years."

Of course, by the time I had successfully navigated three semesters and was in the midst of my own sophomore year I had forgotten all about the ax, for I was feeling good about myself. I had kept up my drinking habits, but only on weekends… until, that is, the seasons changed.

Once winter yielded its grip to the new buds of spring, the rolling hills of Virginia's Piedmont came alive with new spawn and youth's sap running. That was just the thing to prompt three of us one day to borrow a friend's car to go the movies. We left about 8 p.m. We got back the following afternoon. Like the sword of Damocles, "the ax" hung over that escapade.

Being the boys we were, we had no plan. We just wanted to get away for a while and have a few brews. So we drove to the local drive-in movie theater, because you could sit in your car and drink while watching the flick. It was one of Elvis Presley's and not that great, especially without dates. Thus it did not take long for our sap to start running when one of us said the magic words: "Let's go pick up some girls."

We rolled.

In less than 90 minutes we were in midtown Richmond at the dormitory of a small nursing school. It was perfect, an enclave of pulchritude tucked into a corner between a small hospital and an upscale neighborhood of Federalist townhomes. A place of quietude and elegance, it welcomed our presence.

We each knew some of the girls there and tried to call, but no one answered the desk phone.

"Well, what the hell," the ringleader said, "let's just go to the front door, walk in and see what happens."

"Panty-raid?"

"Yeah, if nothing else comes up"– raucous college boy– *sophomoric*– laughter.

But the lobby door was locked by that hour, whatever that happened to be. A light tap on the door would not have worked. We knew from experience that would have brought a quince-faced "house-mother" who would have told us, with dark looks and hands on hips: "The residence hall is closed."

No problem. It was spring, after all, and we could work around something that minor. We scuttled around back to the alleyway serving the modest three-story Georgian brick building and located the rusty old metal fire escape.

A plan formed instantly. It was to get to the second floor, a level above the redoubt of Mizz Quince-face.

"And how exactly do you think we can do that?" our soberest said, "and then what will we do once we get there?"

"Jeez, you old troll, we'll get some dates and sneak back out," said the ringleader.

"Or stage a mini panty raid, right?" ventured I. More raucous laughter.

Either way it was obvious that we'd be welcomed back at school as conquering heroes after this adventure, however it turned out. So we got started.

Another and I hoisted our third co-conspirator, he being smaller than us, to the lowest rung of the ladder that hung down from the fire escape. It was elevated so that not just anybody could pull it down and climb into a girls' dormitory. But its designers didn't know whom they were up against.

Somehow we got our buddy high enough to grasp the lowest rung of the creaky metal ladder.

Once he had it firmly in hand, we began to let him down, pulling the ladder with him. But the horrendous scraping noise the ancient contraption made was like a banshee's screech in a dead-quiet country cemetery.

Soon we heard some real banshees screeching. Trouble, for the sound came from inside the building.

Discretion told us the better part of valor was to make tracks out of there. We released the ladder– which then screeched even more as it left its moorings to crash to the alley's pavement. The screeching and crashing invaded the neighborhood's peace like a Panzer blitzkrieg.

"Holy shit," was our simultaneous response.

We raced to the car, and the providential muses of spring revels were with us. The car was pointed on a one-way street headed away from the perpendicular cross street down which soon came a car of Richmond's finest, red lights flashing. Meanwhile, we drove in the opposite direction and were around the closest Confederate hero's roundabout just in time to merge into an innocent and anonymous line of sedate city dwellers driving up the avenue. We were soon gone with the wind, too.

Since we were westbound and thought it best to get out of town, we headed for Charlottesville. That was irrational. It was 75 miles away and late on a weeknight. We had no plan, but we did have sense enough to know we needed to get something to eat... and best not hereabouts. There were lots of good places to do that in Charlottesville. Never mind the time and distance problem. That's where we were going to have dinner.

We did that, and by the time we had eaten, dawn was breaking, just as another kind of dawn broke over our then-besotted brains. This adventure was beginning to look a little loony. We decided to head for home base. There was a baseball game that afternoon, and we needed to be there.

When we got back, we plopped down on the grass at the baseball field and proceeded to pass out– or "take a nap," as I chose to style it.

The next day, I got up and made it to class as if nothing had happened. After my first class, as always, I went to the campus Post Office to check my mail. Eureka! I could see through the tiny timeworn window that there was something inside my box. A check from home, maybe? No such luck. Instead it was a dreaded "pink slip" from the Office of the Dean of Students. "Mr. Blue, see me immediately," it said. I went.

"I've already talked to some who knew of your little adventure in Mr. Dibbit's car," said the dean, powerfully ensconced behind his polished wooden desk. "So what have you got to say for yourself?"

"Well, sir," I began, my mind scrambling for something rational. That went nowhere.

"We had just gone to the movies, and decided to go get some dates and I guess things kind-of got out of hand."

"I'm surprised that that's the best you can do, Mr. Blue. We thought highly of you when you were offered admission. But I did not expect that you would have taken my admonition about what almost always happens in one's sophomore year literally."

He was not enjoying this, exactly, because I surmised he had been through it many times before. Nevertheless, I offered my apologies. "Sir, it won't happen again. We will do what we need to do in the way apologies and compensation to all."

At that point, I was properly dressed down, the dean having learned all about our adventure, I saying as little else as possible. Yet he knew. And that made sense. The car we had borrowed belonged to one of the dean's *intimes*, a gentleman, scholar, and spy, a studious sort who sang in the college's "glee club," over which the dean exercised virtually exclusive sway. I, an academic loose cannon, and certainly no singer, was fortunate to walk out of his office still a student. I earned social probation for the balance of the year.

But I learned something, and by the following semester, I believe I had managed to mature a bit. I was sobered (but not entirely) by the thought that I had let my family down with my sophomoric antics. And the dean must have sensed that, for he assigned me to another roommate, one who was an "old guy." He had been a student for two years, realized he was not doing well, and dropped out for three years of military service. He returned for his last two years of college. The dean's move was brilliant for under my new roomie's mature influence and cheerful coaching, I made the Dean's List.

Some weeks into that new academic year, I felt as new as the air itself. On one of those perfect crisp fall days, the tree leaves sang as their colors turned to the hues of a new beginning, and I was joined in a walk across campus by the dean. Always the Southern gentleman, he wore a classic tweed jacket, khaki pants and a stylishly shortened bow tie. We spoke as friends, with a feeling of warm academic kinship. I felt exonerated.

In his diplomatic way, he brought up the topic of drinking on campus, encouraging me to own part of the topic by asking: "What do you think about that, Mr. Blue?"

I admitted it would bear watching. "I've had my own, as you know."

"But I can tell you're working on it," he said. "I hope you will continue to do so for we have a problem among a small number. Be careful not to be drawn farther into those circles, for the consequences may not be good."

I accepted and appreciated his warning and concern. I was glad I was there, not just a number, a cipher in some anonymous university. I was to ponder his consideration and never forgot it, because I knew he was right. It would become more important the older I got. But for the moment, it concerned me enough to see what my faith had to say on the matter of drinking.

The normal way to have done that, of course, would have been to talk with the chaplain or consult a Bible. Perhaps subconsciously knowing what I'd learn from that exercise, I undertook my own research. Presbyterian "dissenters" had founded our college in the late 1700s at the start of the American Revolution. The Rare Book Room of the Library contained early treatises on the Westminster Confession of Faith, the constitution of those early dissenters. I would do my research in those tomes.

Dreary hours later, feeling like a cloistered medieval monk amongst the musty old books, about all I could find were what seemed to me to be subtly veiled references to Aristotle's "Golden Mean"– moderation in all things– and I knew I had found my answer. I would go forth, forevermore drinking only "in moderation."

So I toned it down a bit. Fortunately, I convinced myself that I had not crossed the line between "problem drinking" and full-blown alcoholism. "Moderation" would do that for you, I discovered, and I made the Dean's List again. I worked hard and became editor of the student newspaper. By graduation, I felt as though I had been through the valley and emerged on the other side into the larger world a new man. I was encouraged as I turned life's corner to confront that world. But the dean's kindly spoken admonition, and its truth, were ever with me.

CHAPTER TWO

MODERATION IS A FALSE GOD. Just because there were no more rusty crashing fire escapes, and just because I felt good about myself for having done all the next right things, meant not much. Those things had had their day.

I graduated, did my stint in the military, went to work and got married. But deep inside, I suspected all that exterior stuff– painted as it was with "moderation"– was just a façade, a Potemkin's village of a life. Inside the outside was a whiff of ominous warning, an insidious creeping feeling that alcohol was taking over, and it was not going to go quietly into a closet of moldering moderation.

It did not take long for the false god to show itself.

Cars became a big problem, for example. Couldn't do without them, but I crashed them almost routinely. Once I even managed to lose a company rental car, and in the process experienced an extra-marital set-to. But I have no idea exactly how it turned out because my memory went blank during this adventure. If I had admitted then what I secretly suspected, I would have recognized the memory blackout for what it was: a primary indicator of "problem drinking." But that day, I did not have a drinking problem. I had a car problem.

I left the office a bit early and rushed to pick up the rental car– a big Mercury, a shiny black executive-class urban road yacht. I had not driven my car to work that day because I had to go and represent my company at a civic celebration. The press would be there, and my job included media relations. Since there was drinking involved, I got there early, mingled, talked to area business swells and media types, and lo and behold I and an attractive woman TV reporter became an instant item.

She thought it would be a good idea if she and I left and went to an after-event party. I could not have agreed more. So off we went. The after-party party was somewhere, but the trail for me had stopped before we got there. Oh, I went all right, I just did not remember where it was or all that happened.

Professionals tell us that there is an "invisible line" that people who drink too much cross, the Rubicon that leads to active alcoholism. I recalled nothing of the rest of the night except the vague impression that I had a pretty good time. But I believe I crossed my own river of no return. What happened the next day sealed it. In the morning, I got up, put myself together again— I was getting pretty good at that— and drove to my office in my own car.

"Hey, what did you do with the rental car?" my office mate said about mid-morning, and a shock of fear shot through me. How had I gotten home without it? And how had I forgotten where the car was? Was I nuts?

I felt like I'd awakened from a dream of peaceful vistas to a view of hell fires lapping at my feet. My carefully honed corporate knack of diplomacy-under-pressure fled like a chicken from a fox in the henhouse. I realized I just did not know.

"Damn, Ronnie. I forgot all about it. It's still downtown." I had to confess, blanks and all, to my colleague— the beginning of my undoing at that company, as it turned out. But he was a complicit soul, and offered me a way out: "After work we can go downtown and find it. But, man, I'm telling you. This is not good."

We drove downtown and began to retrace my route of the night before. As we got closer to where I thought I had been, paranoia gripped me like a coiling python. I feared the worst. We patrolled a pattern outward from where I last remembered being, and finally found the car. Amazingly barf- and ding-free, it was sedately parked on a graceful avenue under the watchful gaze of one of the city's Confederate memorial statues along Monument Avenue.

My drinking became a daily ritual. One way or another, I would find a way, regardless of increasing imprecations from my wife to stop or at least "control" my drinking. I did not recognize either concept.

Life took on a slow slog of fakery. I learned to hide my drinking– literally. I would stash beer– my drink of choice– in a variety of hiding places, even thick bushes in the borders around our placid suburban home. The subdivision was all folks looking good, kids joyfully playing, moms talking over their gardening, I feeling like some kind of lost loon.

Months of pretended domestic tranquility passed, months of denial and months mimicking someone I was not. My rationalization of moderation became an artifact, like an ancient paperweight on an empty page. Faking it was making me sick, and I did not have a clue about what to do. "To pretend to know, when you do not know," wrote Lao-tzu, 'is a disease." That truth eluded me through a long, baleful, dangerous time.

But I acquired habits that provided cover. I could hide behind them, not realizing I was hiding from myself. On a typical workday, I would leave my office downtown. Sometimes two or three of my colleagues and I would have a drink or two at a nearby bar. That was acceptable behavior. Many people seemed to do that. So that was one hiding place, but only for one or two drinks, no more.

Next, I'd go to my car and begin the 12-mile drive to my home in the suburbs. On the way, I would stop at a convenience store to replenish my dwindling pack of cigarettes. And, oh yes, I'd pick up a couple of beers. Just a couple. Nothing to call attention to myself. Another hiding place. I'd drink them as I drove on, always careful not to quaff a toot when the law lurked.

I might make another stop like that one too, if I needed another behavioral hidey hole, but usually the last stop before home was a neighborhood grocery store about a half mile from the house. In those pre-cell phone days, I would go to a pay phone, call my wife and tell her I was on the way home.

"I'm just leaving downtown," I'd say, "and I thought you might need something from the store."

"Oh, thanks," she'd say. "Yes. Get us some milk, bread, and I need some cigarettes."

I would do just that, and add a six-pack of beer to the list, plus a couple of loose ones. And with the time I had bought by telling her I was "just leaving downtown," I would sit in the car and hide behind the full spread of the afternoon newspaper, fanaticizing myself a secret agent on a case, and drink the extra two.

Those were the days of the ascendency of "Bond... James Bond," agent 007 of Her Majesty's Secret Service. In my deluded muddle I became one with the secretive world of spy craft. I read voraciously of it, and when reality became embarrassing, I mentally shape-shifted to the world of spooks and imagined myself on a mission within it, a self-made schizophrenic.

The months of those days became years. And it was during that time– I don't know exactly when, but I know it happened– that I crossed the invisible line into full-blown alcoholic drinking. Yet I still managed to maintain outward appearances and keep a job, although that was hard work and got harder. It sometimes called for some fancy footwork, a spooky little dance. I was only around 30.

My wife stayed at home and raised our two children. My daughter had preceded my son by almost exactly two years– just as we had planned it. Their mother did a good job, too, especially considering the growing challenge I was becoming. Nevertheless, I carried on, but the edges were beginning to fray.

Financial problems grew. I was trying to manage a household and keep up an increasingly expensive drinking habit at the same time. I played games, shell games, with my income and our assets. I got a second mortgage on the house. I added credit accounts. I began to get behind. That changed the nature of my hiding completely.

Now I wanted to hide from everything, the world. My little family made a beautiful picture, one I cherish to recall to this day, but it became dim like a faded black-and-white photo from the 40s.

I had lost a job but gotten another one, soon to lose it, too. Financial problems rolled in like waves at high tide, and my marriage was on the rocks.

The trip to the end began that day at my parents' home. They were out of town, and I was in full-bore crisis mode. I don't even know why I was there– to "look after things" while they were gone, I think. At least I was grateful for the change of venue. So I sat and began to take inventory of the mess I had made of my young life. By then I was 32, still married with two little kids and a big mortgage. I was about to lose it all. So I decided to call the psychiatrist whom I had seen three years earlier and whom I perceived as my friend. The shock came when he told me he could not help me.

"I know exactly what's happened to you," he said. "You've become a chronic alcoholic and the only thing that can help you now is Alcoholics Anonymous."

Then he hung up on me.

I was stunned. Here I was– finally reaching out for help– and I'm dissed by this shrink. AA for me, of course, was simply out of the question. I slung the phone book across the room, pages flailing. I felt like tearing the room apart. My thoughts went dark. Suddenly giving up, ending it all, made sense. I went to my old room immediately, and very slowly– so slowly it felt otherworldly– I got the magazine I kept there– the one with the three nine-millimeter rounds I had inserted into it, remembering it only took one.

Then I went to get the Luger.

CHAPTER THREE

BUT WHERE WAS IT? I HAD TO GET IT, even though my head was in two places at once. I wanted the gun, but I didn't know why. I did not have the nerve to blow my brains out with it. On the other hand, there was an eerie evil in my mind that I had never known before. It wanted the gun. The evil wanted a nine-millimeter Luger round to explode through my brain. But the Luger was not in its place– thirty years kept in the same place, and now it's not there. Neither were the rifles.

There were things I would later learn. But at the moment, I wanted to know where the Luger was. I searched everywhere. After all, I'd grown up there and I knew all the places it could have been. I searched closet corners, shelves, the attic, behind the oil heater and even underbrush in the yard where I had once played and hid my own secret decoder rings and other treasures. My palms were sweaty. I did not move so much as jerk along, pushed by some dark force I did not dare to pause and ponder.

This pushing energy triggered a war of emotions, desperate and eschatological, like a train hurtling towards split rails dead ahead. It felt unceasing. It would not leave me. But it did. I just stopped my search. I was a big frayed nerve synapse that was not lighting up with any stimulus anymore.

I gave up. The guns were not there anymore, not to be found. I went to the living room, sat in the seat where I had read so much so joyfully over so many years and stared idiotically at the bookcase of wonderful books. I ignored the Bible. But the Bible seemed to speak to me anyway. The Bible would win, too. I believe the very sight of it made me begin a new search, one of my mind. I began to take inventory of where I was, and where I might have just gone.

The search, the unrelenting restlessness of it, turned to a pliability of thought. I began to see options. Not just the wrong way on the one-way street down which I had hurtled. The search itself for the guns seemed to have had a strange calming effect on my angst and loss of rational compass. My life's perspective came back to the present as the eerie evil hissed, and left. At that moment I realized that *my father knew where the guns were*. I remembered how he knew, too.

In my college days when a semblance of academic rigor finally got at least a tenuous hold on me, I had written a paper for a philosophy class whose teacher had participated in trans-oceanic telepathic experiments with students at Oxford University. That was a long time ago– he had been a graduate student in the 20s or early 30s, a time when extra-sensory perception was just beginning to be investigated with some seriousness.

In my own research for a paper for his class, I learned about Dr. J. B. Rhine's work at Duke University's Parapsychology Laboratory,[1] and I tried some telepathic experiments of my own using Duke's "Zener cards."[2] The cards were five playing-card-sized pieces of opaque paper. On each was a simple design– a circle, a cross, three curvy lines, a square and a star.

I discovered that with certain individuals– a former college roommate and my father, to be exact– we could beat probability by large margins in the process of mentally "reading" the randomly selected cards to each other.

My dad and I sat at the dining room table. He held five white cards. He pulled one out and began to gaze at it, obvious concentration showing on what I had come to know as his game face, his accountant's game face, serious concentration.

Directly across from him, I shut my eyes and began to concentrate on the card he held. It was one of the Duke Zener cards. The exercise was a part of a personal experiment, as I finished my paper on paranormal psychology and its effect on ethics.

I began to see a shape, an image floating through my mind. I looked up, and he still showed the accountant's poker face . He said nothing. Finally, after closing my eyes and trying to focus on which of the five possible shapes it could be, I kept "seeing" one in particular: the square.

So, I risked: "It's the square."

"You're right."

We notched another correct identification. Totaling the "corrects" with the "misses" over a couple of weeks of doing this in groups of a half dozen or so, we had nearly 300 tries. And the positives were between 50 and 60 percent– well above probability, according to my research.

I tried this with several people. Only one other, my college roommate, and I could beat probability. The rest were somewhere between ten to fifteen positives. But I thought anything over 50 percent, repeated in different places and at different times of day, was pretty interesting.

I do not doubt that today this experience would be seen as rather unsophisticated, probably even seriously flawed. I knew all of my test-mates well, for example. And there could have been subliminal clues passing between us, especially if I tested the waters by describing what was going through my mind. But my dad... the poker face, no hand movements, nothing. That was different. Nevertheless my mind-reading rationale– while it helped me immensely over the moment at hand– was probably a flawed mental construct. I was getting good at them.

Experiments or not, I now know my father knew what could have happened that baleful day when I went for the Luger. I later learned that he had removed the weaponry from the house and placed it under lock and key in his office downtown. Although we never discussed it, later I could look him in the eye and tell: he had a premonition of what I might try while I was at his house that day. He knew more about my recent history than I thought. Regardless of my imaginings, in truth the bond between my father and me just may have saved my life that day.

When I finally settled down after the telephone encounter with the psychiatrist, I looked at the fact that I had actually thought of blowing my brains out, "ending it all," stopping my dystopian world in mid-orbit. For the first time since my high school years, I began to consider my recent past. I remembered a weathered old book I had squirreled away. I love old books, and this one was a dictionary dated 1828. It was bound in well-worn leather and had my great grandfather's name written in fading ink on the frontispiece. Inside was a piece of paper with handwritten words on it: Plato's famous aphorism: "The life which is unexamined is not worth living."

It had taken me the previous three years to get there, and the car adventure was but one of several milestones on what would be my long march to chronic alcoholism, a line I had crossed by then.

When I was younger, I always recovered quickly; and being relatively glib and a quick study, I could usually talk my way out of tight spots. But by this time, such facile bobbing and weaving had lost its mojo... and more.

Loss of job. Loss of family. Loss of self-worth followed. It took all that for me to learn that the excuse of depression I had once embraced was really an extended family lie, and that these events were actually caused by something. Oh, I was convinced that the culprits were all external: wife, job, weather, whatever. It didn't make any difference, as long as they were not my doing. The truth, of course, was that those consequences were caused by a very strong depressant drug: alcohol. "We have met the enemy," said Pogo, a long-time favorite newspaper cartoon character, "and he is us."

When the truth finally bored through my mental defenses— ramparts built up through years of fanciful thinking— I felt helpless because the obvious implication was that I would have to stop drinking, give up what had become a beloved old friend. The thought of stopping actually frightened me. My core went cold at the concept. How could anybody ever do that?

Stop? Why, it would be... ungentlemanly, I sputtered to myself. Behaving as a "Southern Gentleman" was not something to be trifled with. The ability to "drink like a gentleman" was prized in the culture of my upbringing. Such traditions were to be upheld, and principles like "work hard, play hard" were to be maintained. After all, strange things had happened to folks who did not drink.

"How much more stupid can you get, Doug," I asked myself , staring at my books. Scarlett O'Hara got it right:

"Tomorrow is another day."

Deal with it.

I began to inventory my memories and repeatedly saw the bizarre effects of alcohol abuse. I even had a passing acquaintance once who said he did not drink because his daddy– as if stepping off the pages of a Faulkner novel– had died in a hatchet fight while on a three-day binge.

The story of how my erstwhile friend's father died in an alcoholic binge convinced my friend to never drink frightened me. The threat it posed to my own cloaked behavior is why the acquaintance then became a passing one. That's one way I dealt with the undeniable facts of alcoholic abuse in a life... I just blew it off the table and defriended the guy who told me.

That day beside the bookcase, I realized for the first time he was probably trying to help me by sharing his own story, a precious commodity, I would come to learn.

Another time, I met the grandfather of a drinking buddy. "Paps" drank moonshine while holed up in his "office," a tiny room in the basement of a cavernous yet genteel deteriorating Victorian mansion in a magnolia-filled Southern town, surrounded by dozens of homemade wooden shelves, all holding sealed Mason jars of his feces.

Connecting that dot– an old alcoholic who saved his doo-kee– came up from my memory vault, the one I thought closed, and slapped me in the face just as I spotted Goebbel's Diaries on the bookshelf. Hitler's PR guy– the one who had made "The Big Lie" a part of Nazi Germany's national policy– came back from the scaffold where he died to teach me a lesson about my own Big Lie.

Those things and more I had stuffed into that vault in my mind– a place where the sun never shone and my thinking thumped around, like an adult's "closet monster." Then and there I came to understand that my vault was really a part of a rapidly sickening soul but nonetheless a place God had saved for me, if I ever admitted I needed to live a life examined.

I had denied hundreds of memories of the things I did as I nurtured my illusory Southern Gentlemen.

The blackouts were the worst. *I did things I did not remember doing. What were they?*

The fear was as cold as a stone in winter, so strong I dared not ask anyone about anything. The blackouts haunted me. They were ephemera that came and went, ugly packets of corrupted data, passing like dark wraiths across a moonless moor.

The only out I had– and this was rare– was when one of my hale-fellows, well-met would say– and this really happened– stuff like "Hey, Doug how about that safari you led? That was great. We ought to do that again."

"Yeah, that was great," I would say, wondering what he was talking about. But in such times of good-ol'-boy banter, sometimes the truth would rise up from the vault.

The "safari" I led was a kind of conga-line through a nearby cemetery in the middle of the night. I got a bed sheet and wrapped it around me like some kind of guru, and led this bizarre hopping, dancing procession through a cemetery, a line of mostly young women behind me. The guys thought it was... I don't know what they thought, really. But it earned me the sobriquet "Bwana."

But that was early. And rare. And certainly fed my own shame, an emotion which I knew no cure for. Shame on top of fear on top of the terror of unknowing became like plaque in arteries, goop that slowly built up... until it blocked life. I had a close call.

Sticky fears joined a paranoia that others would figure out what was going on with me. They became fears of fire fanned by demons that made the drinking become a necessity to quench, to medicate, and ameliorate, as much as possible. They were dark fires, lies, hallucinatory tactics; but I willed myself forward in spite of them.

That's why, when my wife was making her case for me to return to "moderate" drinking, her best point was: "You don't have the willpower to stop." She never realized that I was actually exercising massive willpower to continue drinking under such challenging conditions and against such flimsy logic. The old "willpower" argument meant nothing to me. "In War: Resolution. In Defeat: Defiance..." wrote Sir Winston Churchill in *The Gathering Storm*. I wanted to engrave it on a plaque and put it on my dresser.

I became defiant. Yet the dark fires kept driving me to the very edge of sanity, to things I had vowed never to do: To lie. To marital infidelity. To skate on the edge of the law, even to the point of entertaining murder.

Infidelity is not as great as I thought it would be. I was expecting an encounter like James Bond's with Pussy Galore, his paramour in *Goldfinger*. What I got instead was closer to supermarket tabloid, too complicated and everybody would know. Oh, and never mind the inability to see outcomes clearly. And moral implications? They meant nothing to me back in the day of high-end alcoholism. The concept of fidelity sagged under the sway of some sort of law of diminishing domestic returns. I faced a dilemma: infidelity versus fidelity, a faceoff with fast-fading prospects. One night after a few toots too many I set out to clarify the issue.

Hangovers had become problems, because by then I did not know what to expect. I would usually awake in a state of transient memory lapse. My infidelity was like that– one of those mornings.

I was lying in a strange bed– nice, but not mine.

"What now," I thought, knowing that I would remember soon, because there was someone else I the bed with me.

First I managed to open one bleary eye. The other was stuck shut. The inside of my mouth felt like moss on a forest floor. The air was clear. The smells clearly feminine. A non-smoker?

But with one eye now open, I was shocked not immediately to recognize where I was. How had I gotten here? And where was here?

Sometimes in the lives of active alcoholics, things like this happen— so many times, in fact, it becomes routine, a part of life, just like mouth moss or losing large domestic automobiles.

Remembrance always returns, however, sometimes with shocking suddenness, and as I turned over and saw the backside of a woman's blonde head of hair, I fell headlong into reality. Needless to say it was not my wife's head of hair, an attractive dark auburn-red. No doubt, then, about recent history: my blonde friend and I had spent the night together.

How it had come to that and what had happened crept back into my muddled mind like mud oozes down a creek bank in the rain.

Things had started innocently enough. My lady friend and I were business colleagues. We were working late together. We liked each other. She was newly divorced. I was surely about to be. We both liked to drink. We did, and business soon yielded to nature. One thing led to another and the more we drank the more apparent it became that this was going to be the night we did something about the evening's subtext.

"Let's go have a drink and talk about it," said I, "maybe the Hanover House?"

"I'd like that," she said, with a half-smile revealing a subtle signal, one that reminded me of a Rose of Sharon's first late-spring bud.

That's how it started.

My wife and kids had once again gone to visit her mother at the river. This was becoming routine, the sure sign of a rapidly deteriorating marriage. Of course I didn't see it then. I sublimated it. I couldn't look at it. So into the vault it went. I had slowly slipped into an unreal way of life. One that denied. One like a young boy who thinks he can put on his Superman cape and jump off the roof of his house. One that had come to reflect the three worst things alcoholics do.

Those three things are: lie, cheat, and steal. They are a collective common denominator for advanced alcoholic behavior. At least that's what it looks like to me as I reflect with the unvarnished and unsparing honesty borne of a burning desire to get well and stay that way. Truth carries a cost.

When I was able to open the second eye that morning, and get rid of the mouth moss, I rousted my friend and we began what people in the business world called a "postmortem" on the night before.

After dinner we had gone to her apartment, a cozy affair nestled in suburban anonymity and surrounded by trees and plants in full spring growth. We had a few more drinks and that's when memory began to fade. Neither of us was real sure what happened next. Too much alcohol is a fickle friend of remembrance. I had no idea what happened, if anything, but I suspected it had.

With morning, we got ourselves together. I took a quick shower put my clothes on. I went to the kitchen and tried to make coffee. She followed. We were drinking coffee when she said, "You look like you could use something else." She got up, left the room and came back with a pill bottle. "Have one. It's Librium."

After my Librium and coffee and some relatively irrelevant chitchat, we parted ways.

Experiences like that exemplify the potential for dysfunction and wrongdoing most alcoholics have. It can be hard to draw straight lines between those behaviors, but at the heart of them is self-deception, a tragic consequence in all-too-many cases.

"How many drinks have you had today?" the police officer investigating a fender-bender would ask.

"Oh, just a couple," I'd say. "I just left a business meeting that ended with a few cocktails," I would say. And now I'm on my way home."

Many times in those days police officers would buy that rather than work through the detail and hassle of charging me with driving under the influence. I could end up with a warning, or at worst a ticket for "impaired driving."

The day came though when I got two reckless driving tickets in separate jurisdictions within a matter of about three hours. In one instance I scrapped a wall, in another I had hit a parked car. In both cases I was driving rental vehicles. And I was drinking. This was real trouble because two reckless driving tickets within a year, I believe it was in that day, would result in a suspended driving license. But on the same day– only three hours apart? I was doomed.

Things were not as strict then as they are today, however; and my saving grace was that the two incidents were in separate counties. That meant separate courts. And digital divining rods had not yet arrived. Today, of course, I probably would have lost my license and more.

My lawyer got one reduced to "improper driving," and the other resulted in a single reckless driving conviction. My license was saved, and I got to go to "Safe Driving" school. But I did have to deal with two rental car companies and pay for the damage I had caused. Such is life when one lives in thrall to a drug-led life.

In my case I had developed a warped-reality mode of thinking in which what I actually did was what I believed most everybody else was doing too– perhaps the ultimate moral equivalency, a wonderland in which I could make six plus three equal sixty-three.

Drawing lines among behaviors was one way I allowed myself to be fooled. For example, for years, tennis was my game, and if an opponent's ball had nicked the outside of the line, I'd graciously give my opponent the point. So I was strictly honest in that and in other matters. But when it came to certain other behavior– and what I needed to keep my self-image in focus– my dodge was John McEnroe's famous line: "You have got to be kidding me."

I weaseled on expense reports and my taxes, if I had a reasonable chance of getting away with it. Extra-marital dalliance was different. Yet there I was that morning. Another line crossed, I had dallied.

Drinking became a vicious circle. Values like truth and a clear conscience looked like research rats scuttling through a maze.

One day I was taking an innocent elevator ride in the office building where I worked. The building dated from the late twenties and so did its elevators. They rather groaned their ups-and-downs than whisked them. And when mine jerked to a stop at the executive floor, I straightened my tie.

But on board came Boze, an old friend from college, appropriately suited for visitation to an executive suite, grinning ear-to-ear with his tie straightened, too.

"Doug, my man. How you been? Good to see you," he said shaking hands collegially but a tad too enthusiastically. He was selling something.

"Fine," I lied. I was always "fine" in those days.

"Great. I'm in the banking business now. Here's my card and as matter-of-fact here's a loan application, too," he said with a quick wink. "Stick it in your desk drawer and when you need anything give me a call. I'll fix you up."

And that I did. I discovered the miracle of ninety-day notes. Before plastic had become the coin of the realm, ninety-day notes were tailor-made for alcoholics— at least those who still held down jobs.

With a ninety-day note, you agreed to borrow, say, $500 for ninety days. But at the end of the term if you didn't have $500, you could pay your banker the interest on $500 for the period. I stretched that to its limit, several times over.

Add to that the check-kiting schemes my best friend, a stock-broker, and I created. The plot was planned over beers one day after work.

"Float," Al said.

"Float what?" I said.

"Float is the answer to our cash-flow problem," my longtime friend and drinking-buddy said. "It's a banking term for the time it takes for funds to pass between banks."

"I know that, stupid, but what's it got to do with running out of drinking money before pay days?" I asked.

"We usually both run out of money about three days before our paydays, right? So we can use float between banks to make ourselves little loans."

What a concept, thought I. I knew about float but had never seen it quite that way.

"Talk to me," I said.

"Simple. We deal with separate banks. I write you a check for $25 today. You deposit it in your bank today and later write a $25 check to "cash" at your grocery store. You've got $25.

Two days later, you get paid and write me a check for $25 which I deposit right away, and my first check is covered because it took that long for it to pass through the process at Bank A, the grocery store and Bank B and get back to my account, which now has your check registering as a credit. See?"

I processed that concept in about 10 seconds and my mind lit up like the White House Christmas tree. Santa Claus was coming to town.

"Outstanding," said I. "Let's do it."

We did. It worked. For a day or two at the most, that is. But soon we had refined the concept by both opening checking accounts in small, rural banks, preferably ones with really old accounting systems. So then we had Banks A, B, C, and D– two of which were small and out-of-town. That added to the float factor in those days well before the virtually instantaneous data-transfer of today.

Our kites would fly from A to C, to B, and to– or some variation thereof– and cash out the checks involved before our "settlement" day arrived.

So it came to be that we could each make it to pay day without missing a single drink. But it could get pretty confusing, and if one of us had a bad enough hangover on kite-flying days, operational chaos would ensue, the whole chain would crash in a big-city minute, and the piper would come a'calling.

That was easily solved, though. We had well-honed talking points by then and could explain, apologize and fix the "inadvertent" error, let a week pass, and do it all over again. And then, there were still 90-day notes, too. Life was good.

All the while these ugly farces were going on, the truth still stood, waiting for its day, immutable, annoyingly like the 800-pound gorilla in the middle of the living room floor that everyone pretended wasn't there. Little did I know, of course, that I was on track for a frightening confrontation with the gorilla.

CHAPTER FOUR

AN ANCIENT MIRROR IN A DIMLY-LIT Victorian House can be a frightening thing. It was nothing like Alice's Looking Glass, but I was in my own Wonderland and circumstances were leading to an otherworldly experience with that very mirror.

Denial was a prominent and deadly characteristic of my sixteen years of drinking. Most deceptive was the devilment denial would cause, as down the rabbit-hole I went. It played out over several months in the early 70s— perhaps two-thirds of the way down the path, yet moving inexorably to that mirror.

Nestled in a brick-walled courtyard of one of Richmond's storied Fan District homes— elegant vintage townhomes lining streets that splayed out in a fan when viewed on a map— lay the small patio area of an English basement apartment where my friend Al and his wife lived. It was an elegant place to meet. We were surrounded by the palpable 19th Century ambiance of plush gardens, overhanging willows and the aura of Monument Avenue near where my old hero "Jeb" Stuart has his circle— a traffic circle around the triumphalist "Lost Cause" statue of him on his horse, Virginia. There Al and I— when we weren't creating check-kiting schemes— concluded that the best thing we could do would be to move to Australia.

After all...

"There is a place. Like no place on Earth. A land full of wonder, mystery, and danger! Some say to survive it: You need to be as mad as a hatter.[3]*"*

I heard the Mad Hatter's whispers to me, as I embraced the possibilities the

Land Down Under held. Our studies confirmed that it was like no place on earth... to us, anyway; but being rationally mad meant we first needed some facts to justify moving there.

So Al, beer in one hand, brought forth a popular business journal's story reporting that the government of Australia was attempting to recruit bright young business men– that would've been us, of course– to help their country develop further.

We assembled pounds of literature– chamber of commerce stuff, newspaper articles, testimonials from brave entrepreneurs– which we would pore over while our dutiful wives poured drinks for us all. This was "due diligence" at its best, and anything for a drink in those days.

A few troublesome details kept getting in the way: for one, my ongoing obligation to my Army Reserve regiment; and for another, questions like, well, what would we *do* in Australia, anyway? We wasted hours on this exercise, all affirming the greener-grass theory, but truly adding up to nothing more than what I came to know as "the geographic cure."

Cure for what? Certainly not depression, my long-time artful dodge that empowered stasis and therefore an excuse for my behavior. The storyline got pretty thin after a while. Wonderland evanesced. So did my thinking. The end was near.

It stretched over eight or nine months in 1973 and '74. It felt interminable, because my life itself seemed to be on probation. The Luger returned to mind, while I, nursing my other addiction, cigarettes– Marlboros, of course– once more entertained escapist thoughts. The path was not smooth but full of "thorns and thistles," just as God promised Adam; and I had gone astray, just as Dante chronicled.

Meanwhile, the mirror waited in the gloom.

One morning in the summer of 1973 I awoke with a very bad feeling, and this was not a hangover. I had gotten into a back-and-forth drinking mode. I'd drink a few days. Then I would refrain for a few. I thought I might be able to control it that way. Fear drove it. I was beginning to notice subtle blotches on my face, slight reddish areas. They frightened me, hypochondriac that I was. I knew something had changed. I also knew it was bad. But I didn't have a rational idea of what to do about it. There were so many other things going on, the least of which were kite-flying and automobile-driving.

I was about to lose my job– probably the best I had ever had, at least financially. It was about to happen because of the same mindset with which I met the reddish blotches– denial. My supervisor had called me in one day a few weeks earlier and confronted me.

"We think you're drinking too much, Doug," he said. It was the "We" that felt like a sucker punch in the gut. "We?" and who might they be? They became dark shadows that moved about with me, just out of sight behind and beside me.

"...and we think you need to do something about it," he continued. "Do you have any thoughts about that?"

I told him I would think about it.

"Yes," I said. "Give me a chance to talk it over with my wife."

And I did. I knew that there were places one could go, hospitals that treated alcoholism. My boss heartily agreed that I should go to one.

"You would not be the first from here, you know," he said. "Some of the folks you work with and know have been through this same exercise, and it worked. There's no stigma to this in our company. The company would pay for it, too," he said. "And you'd have a job when you came back."

He was clearly on my side. We liked each other, and worked well together. Hindsight's always twenty-twenty, but unfortunately I was not seeing well that day. He really wanted me to work the program so I could stay there. I was frightened, however. I felt completely alone. Something from my past was holding me back, something I could not name, something in the family dynamics. I just did not know.

"We have long experience in dealing with issues like yours, Doug. We can make some recommendations for treatment. But I want to give you a chance to talk to your doctor and family and decide what you will do."

"Sure," I said. "Thanks."

I felt underwater in a strange cove. I did not have any idea what I was doing. But I pretended I did. As my wife and I sat on our sofa— kids playing happily in a back room— I made the mistake once more of believing myself. Really, I was frozen, trapped between what a still, small voice told me was right and the magic words my wife then spoke: "Going to one of *those places*," she said, "would be a cop-out."

I did nothing, thinking she was right. A "cop out." Yes it was. I saw my opening, my second chance. It was short lived, because I told my boss what my wife and I had decided. "We talked and think that hospitalization would be a cop-out."

About two weeks went by, and then about two one afternoon, it happened.

"Doug can you join me?" my boss said. "Right away. It's important."

"Sure," I said, and I felt the stabbing feeling in my gut of something as strange to me as a blue Moon: reality.

I sat on the chair next to his desk. With no hesitation, he said: "This concerns your discharge."

Truth slapped the face of my denial. I knew this was coming, the moment of reckoning. The evidence was there. I had sat down with two colleagues at lunch in our cafeteria that day and they ignored me, barely acknowledging even my presence. I felt that like a knife being twisted inside of me. *They knew*.

By two-thirty, I was seeing the company doctor for a final checkup. I had removed all my personal possessions from my desk as my boss watched. The office door was locked. But everybody knew what was happening. By three o'clock I was out the door, no longer employed. It was a beautiful April day in 1973.

CHAPTER FIVE

A WEEK LATER, I CONSIDERED ENDING IT ALL, again, a good job just lost, no prospects, family threatened, financial pressures mounting. I knew just what I'd do, too.

I went to the bank.

It was one of those boxy "modern" architectural atrocities on the periphery of a shopping center surrounded by a massive, hot, black asphalt parking lot. I went into the bank and asked the manager if I could see the vault. "Certainly, sir," she said. (I was dressed up, fresh haircut, no hangover. I had reformed.. for a moment, anyway.)

"What would you be needing the safe-deposit box for?" she said.

"Oh, well, things," I stammered. She had caught me off guard as I had no intention of renting a box. I had something else in mind. "Papers, you know, important papers, deeds... you know," I said. "That kind of stuff."

"Fine, then this should work for you."

Bank Lady didn't realize she was dealing with the Mad Hatter's avatar. I did not react. Instead, without answering her, I left. I had found out what I wanted to know—the location of the heavily walled vault.

I drove to the far end of the parking lot, noting the distance on my odometer. It was just over a quarter of a mile. Next I estimated what my car would do in a drag race, a quarter of a mile.

I would be back later that night, after all the customers and workers had gone home. Then I'd roar across the center's empty lot like Willie Nelson going out in a "blaze of glory." I'd hit the solid vault side of the bank building at exactly a 90-degree angle, and thereby do myself in.

Satisfied with my plan, the bank-vault ploy went into the other vault, the one in my mind, but close to the surface, ready for V Day.

...which never came. A few beers at lunch got my thinking back on a more positive path. I'd learned long ago that alcohol could clarify my thinking like that. Positive thinking lasted until the blackout that would follow later.

In the progression of alcoholism, "suicidal ideation" is a toxic tocsin. Beyond it lay The Bottom, a Stygian place with only two endgames: recovery or death—sometimes quick, most times slow and baleful.

I am saddened that by far most people who abuse alcohol or drugs are on the latter road and on the road they will stay... until the end.

I became incapable of thinking about consequences or making life-or-death choices. For several months through the end of 1973 and into 1974, I endured The Bottom.

In Tennessee Williams' *Cat on a Hot Tin Roof*, in a scene set in an upstairs bedroom of a classic Southern antebellum mansion, Brick, the protagonist— his glory days as a high school football star now long since passed— has become alcoholic. Brick explains to his wife, Maggie the Cat, that he must drink until he got "the click," the point where alcohol defeats realism and induces a false feeling of well-being, and there Brick would find peace. Except he had gotten to the point where he could not reach "the click" anymore.[4]

I remember the beautiful day in 1973 when I realized neither could I get "the click" anymore. There was no way out. Even in the midst of a glorious sunlit Virginia summer I had come to love, I began to walk in perpetual twilight, storm clouds menacing, in a mood all gray. Each step became tedious and fearsome. I thought anew about getting the Luger. Although still not in its place, I would see it again.

PART TWO

War, Ghosts and Basketball

CHAPTER SIX

MARCH 8, 1946 DAWNED DANK AND DRIZZLY, in Richmond, Virginia. I was almost four-and-a-half years old, and I was looking forward to a parade. Now it looked like my parade was about to be rained on.

The drizzle became more heavy mist as my mother, my grandmother and I crossed North Boulevard at Monument Avenue, the intersection that Stonewall Jackson oversees. Dressed up in my little-boy-of-the-40s blue sailor suit, I recall a vague feeling that we were going to something very important, and that the parade was just a sidelight. At my age– and perhaps the reason I recall the event in the first place– I knew that drizzles had a way of turning into rain, and rain could mess up your day, especially when you were expecting something as exciting as a parade– a *parade* with soldiers, bands, horses and clowns. Perhaps my expectations were not as high as they deserved to be, given what I was about to witness.

My grandmother, in the mellifluous Georgia accent of her own upbringing, encouraged me about the gray mist. After all, she had come 250 miles from her home in Elizabethtown, North Carolina– a place that had become a second childhood home for me– just to be here with us, so I knew something significant was about to happen. I was excited, despite the lowering skies.

We went and stood beside the balustrade near the imposing, classically columned, main entrance to the First Baptist Church. First I saw a large cohort of

Richmond's finest on horseback and rumbling motorcycles flashing red lights. Following the police was an open limousine with two men waving to people.

"Who are they?" I wondered.

One brandished a big cigar as if in tribute to this old tobacco town; the other wore a military uniform and flashed a famous grin. It was much later that I would appreciate the monumental significance of the two. They were the leaders of the Western Alliance– Sir Winston Churchill and General Dwight D. Eisenhower.

Escorted by Virginia Governor William Tuck, who appeared in news photos of the day to be wedged between the two in the back of the open limousine– his escortees were each good-sized men– the world-famous pair was on its way to the Virginia Capitol where Churchill addressed the Virginia General Assembly. His talk followed the British Prime Minister's historic, controversial, and soon-to-be famous "Iron Curtain" speech at Westminster College in Fulton Missouri.[5]

Meanwhile my parade was fast dissolving in sporadic rain. Umbrellas blossomed then closed– only to open again as large crowds looked on. I stood on the balustrade looking for the real parade. The two old guys were interesting, but my show was soon completely rained out and I thought about home, wondering if maybe the garbage men would come around today. I always watched for the garbage men.

But I was there that day to see Churchill and Eisenhower. My father later taught me about Victory in Europe and Churchill's speech. I learned that he foretold yet another war, the "Cold War," the one soon to come with the Soviet Union behind the grim curtain being lowered across Europe and Eurasia.

On that day, I was confirmed as a war baby.

As a little boy's memory dawned, war was there, palpable, close and scary– nothing like the wars of today– insular affairs that seem to yield monuments to politicians and egos while bravery and sacrifice play second fiddle from afar. No. My war was the real deal.

Doubtless its presence affected my future. It weighed upon the lives of all. But there was still nothing in the trajectory of my growing-up– nor in my earliest memories– pointing to the events that would years later find me face-to-face with the proverbial 800-pound gorilla that no one would talk about. Nor was there anything to portend the feeling I was to have years hence of the hot breath of a demonic presence behind me.

In retrospect, many people assumed the place I'd gotten myself into was the product of a broken home, or some secret dysfunction. But that was not the way it was.

There was an intimacy to families in the 40s, a cohesion even I felt as a little fellow. We moved together as a clan, against whatever came our way. I felt that, as a war baby, and carried the feeling forward. I remember bits and pieces from the time I was three, unusual yes, and most remembrances were more like impressions than solid memories. Nevertheless sometime between three and four, some began to stand out.

We lived in Richmond's near West End, now known as "the Museum District" because of its proximity to the Virginia Museum of Fine Arts and the Virginia Historical Society– grand classically styled edifices that dominate the neighborhood. On the block just to the west of that property, where also lie the Daughters of the Confederacy's offices, library and museum, was Benedictine High School, a military academy. Every Friday the cadets would form up at the close of studies and parade through our neighborhood with a full military band. My mother would take me to watch, and that's why I loved parades. They knew how to do them right.

Our little apartment's kitchen had a small table and chairs. Something good was often cooking on the gas-fired stove. My favorite was my mother's own home-made spaghetti, a treat she had learned to make from my grandmother's cook, "Bet," who made the best cookies anywhere. A warmth permeated it all, and many of my earliest memories were set in that kitchen.

There I would "help" my folks crush cans and bend up coat hangers. Recycling was routine during the war that then raged in Europe and the Pacific. We were all vested in its success, not indifferent to the world around us.

The kitchen led into a large living room with windows to the outside along the street-front portico, and the side windows overlooked an alley that divided us from a building and parking lot next door.

When I heard the trash truck roar up the side alley, I ran to that side window with the impetuous glee of a little child who just could not wait for what followed– trash pickups. I loved them. They were major entertainment for me in those pre-TV days. The men dumped the trash into the backs of large, loud trucks. A big pneumatic plate shoved the trash farther into the backs of the trucks where it disappeared. I was fascinated by the process, and from that moment on I knew what I wanted to be when I grew up: a garbage man.

Another thing I remembered was weather reports on the radio. The radio was on often at our house during the War, and I was fascinated by the weather. A sonorous voice reported: "Here is the weather for Richmond and vicinity." Except I heard it as "Richmond and The Cinity." For the longest time I wondered about the Cinity. Where was this Cinity?

There were other times– night times– when my folks put blankets over the windows to the outside. I understood that was a part of living in a city during a world war, just as collecting pieces of metal in the kitchen, saving "rationing stamps" for gas and tires for our late-30s-model Chevrolet sedan. Covering up windows in the night, I learned, was required during "blackouts," exercises we city dwellers had to go through at a time when Nazi submarines trolled the Eastern seaboard. And if Great Britain fell, the Luftwaffe and V2s could come here next.

These were a child's view of wartime in the homeland. I was born seven days before the Japanese attacked Pearl Harbor– not a so-called "Boomer" but a tiny sentient part in a worldwide struggle for control over others.

I have a black-and-white photograph of me in my little "stroller" when I was probably three or so. I'm on the sidewalk with Richmond's Monument Avenue behind me. We are near Stonewall Jackson's statue. But the most dramatic thing about this photo is the expression on my face. It is very serious, the expression of one much older, a reflection of a little guy who'd absorbed the tensions of growing up during a war, I believe.

My uncles were away. One was a machine-gunner aboard a B-17 bomber. Another was in an artillery unit which traversed Europe after D Day. And a third was a B-17 pilot. They all came home after the war, but my uncle who manned the machine gun had a cauliflower ear from an explosion that must have been way too close for comfort.

My own father was away much of the time, too. He was with a defense contractor and exempt from overseas duty, but still gone for long stretches. Family and home life became split between our apartment in Richmond and my maternal grandmother's home along the Cape Fear River in Bladen County, North Carolina— the place of my roots. So I experienced the dichotomy of a city's wartime tension set against the placid culture of small-town Carolina life with the kind of folks I sprang from. One period from that time— truly a treasure— stands out in my memory.

CHAPTER SEVEN

I REGRET NOT ASKING THE OLD FOLKS what it was like when they were young. Now most of them are gone, and I have become one of them. Ironic, isn't it, that none of the young folks are asking me what it was like? Maybe they know that if they hang out with me long enough I will volunteer some stories. I do, of course. It's in my genes. I heard and experienced such richness as a child that I think today I share tales with my children and grandchildren in gratitude to my forbearers.

"Bet," Elizabeth Lesesne, was my first and favorite story-teller. Probably because of the cookies, she was my buddy from my earliest memory. But more memorable than cookies were her stories. She worked for fifty-four years for my grandmother, a patrician daughter of the Old South. And, although a bit taciturn, Bet would occasionally let fly with some real doozies. Like the time she told me about seeing Colonel McDowell on the back porch.

Colonel McDowell had built the splendid white-columned house my mother grew up in. It was a grandly proportioned and porticoed example of traditional Southern neo-classical architecture and in fact it still is— upgraded by its latest owners and still nestled among the sweet-gum trees and live oaks festooned with Spanish moss.

But the Colonel had built it just after the Late Unpleasantness— a genteel term in the 40s for the Civil War— in which he served. By the time Bet saw him, he had been dead for many years.

Yes. The old house was thought to be haunted– a concept that caused me no end of glee in those pre-TV days before the secular materialism of the later 20th Century began to dull things spiritual, or stretch them to ridiculous extremes.

A haunted house in my old family! What great good fortune had befallen me.

The stories grew over the years, I noticed, in direct proportion to how much I egged the old folks on about them. They hinted at booted footfalls on the stair steps late at night and noises in the attic, even muffled sounds suggesting chains being dragged– especially on muggy Southern coastal nights in the years before air conditioning when the trees' susurrations in the night provided the only relief from the heat. There were whispered appearances. Shadows shifted suspiciously. Mysterious mists evanesced. The Moon came and went behind clouds, and things moved ever so slightly.

My grandmother was widowed when I was a baby, so I never knew my maternal grandfather. Some years later, after my youngest uncle grew up, my grandmother built a smaller, more practical house on the edge of the hill which led down to the Cape Fear River.

That hill was a wonder in itself– sharks' teeth from the time this land was primordial beach, arrowheads hewn by its original occupants, Minié balls from Civil War skirmishes, artifacts and even graves from the Revolutionary War– they were all there.

To this day, the monumental trees with their Spanish moss hanging from gentle limbs still grace the property. I had my favorite spot under their canopy in shade redolent of sweet gum and my grandmother's carefully cultivated chrysanthemums and gardenias. She was an avid gardener and won awards for her flowers, once even creating a new hue to one of the two. I can't remember which. I was a helper then but not yet a creator. There were neighbors too, of course– cousins and Dr. Glenn, who owned the only cow I ever knew.

And there was also Patrick.

Patrick had lived thereabouts in the 18th Century. His grave had been discovered and disturbed when the telephone company dug a hole for its pole at the corner of my grandmother's lot. People said his spirit wandered about the property at night, as if in search of its home. Bet said Patrick would sometimes move the wicker lawn furniture around at night. Dogs howled at nothing you could see. And very late on a summer's night, I would look out the window, hear a million little creatures' night cacophony on the river hill, feel the warm gentle breezes and watch the Moon-fed shadows play tricks with my mind's eye, and I knew the stories about Patrick were true.

In those halcyon days, I learned where the phrase "like a chicken with its head cut off" came from.

Sundays were special. First, we always went to church— a monumental undertaking, There was much hustle and bustle, face-scrubbing, and gentle reminders to us kids to mind our manners. Then off we'd go to the Methodist church where my maternal family's roots were. The place where I had been baptized as a baby was the church's original building, now a museum— a plain white frame structure with a slave gallery. When I was younger I wanted to know why we could not sit "up there," only to be hushed in that peculiarly Southern manner that made the balcony a place of either particular reverence or remindful of something which was not discussed. I never knew which then, but I do today.

At church there were always many friendly folk, cousins, neighbors, townsfolk, farmers and all. The services were traditional. Nineteenth Century hymns accompanied by an organ's deep resonance and a large choir stirred the soul. Everyone dressed up. Behavioral constraints were in effect, and woe to the kid who dared test them.

One time, in the middle of what must have been a particularly riveting sermon, my crayon dropped to the floor. I followed. Once there, I discovered that I could crawl under the pew to the one behind me where some of my cousins were.

One of them and I explored places together, particularly in the ancient forest on the river hill. We imagined one day coming upon a chest full of pieces of eight stashed there by the infamous Edward Teach– Blackbeard!– who had been known to ply the waters of the Cape Fear in the 1700s.

Under-pew exploration was prohibited, short-lived, and I always got caught. But another experience would soon befall me that day, one that would eclipse even a hunt for Blackbeard's treasure.

Once church was over, we went home, and the longest ritual of Southern life would commence: preparing for Sunday dinner. It seemed to me longer than the last Ice Age. Marked by peculiar rituals, I was about to witness the most memorable of them all. It was horrible and fascinating at the same time, an experience etched on my young mind. It was a sight most kids today will never have, one just as gone-with-the-wind as Tara.

My buddy Bet invited me to go with her to "pick out a chicken."

My grandmother maintained a small chicken coop adjacent to her house. It was surrounded by a fence, and sometimes I went there to commune with the chickens. I learned where eggs came from. The chickens became friends of mine. But this Sunday was different. Bet and I were going to "pick one out."

To eat.

Once this reality dawned on me, I went into an altered state of being, one I was of course to need to experience, because there came many times later in life when the same attitude towards life's realities would help me get through times of challenge. I soldiered on, shelving my feelings.

I got to stand on a tree stump to watch. Bet got her hatchet, and we "picked one out." A quick, unenthusiastic "Unhh" being my murmur of agreement.

It was one of those times that probably didn't take but a few seconds to unfold, but it seemed stretched by the sort of slow-motion with which fast actions of immense consequence often seem to proceed.

Bet took the hapless chicken. She stretched its neck across an adjacent tree stump. She raised the hatchet high over her head. And then she swung it down quickly and expertly onto the chicken's elongated neck. There was a "kumpf" sound. And the next thing I knew, the damned thing was running around— headless— blood squirting out of the hole its head once covered.

I was transfixed. Forget the War. This was great... and awful at the same time. It ran around helter-skelter like that. I cowered in fear thinking it might run to me, somehow perceiving our friendship and that I might be able to find its head and put it back on. Or worse, that it might blame me, and like some zombie closet monster, "get" me. Instead— after what seemed to be an impossibly long time— the chicken, the rest of him anyway, plopped to the ground, twitched a bit and then lay still.

Endlessly later, when we finally gathered for Sunday dinner, we invoked God's blessing with thanksgiving, and partook of all manner of fresh vegetables and hot biscuits with real butter. We drank iced tea— not sweetened, by the way. You had to sweeten to taste yourself in the real South. The sweet-tea fetish we see today is just a result of some latter-day retail aberration.

Sunday dinner was always a grand event. The setting was a traditional dining room with classic sideboards flanking dark-hued finely grained wooden cabinetry. French doors led onto a "sun room" that overlooked my grandmother's prized chrysanthemums and geraniums. Beyond that lay the forest leading down the hill to the Cape Fear. The furnishings were Queen Anne astride an ornate oriental rug. Beneath it at the head of the dining-room table where my grandmother presided was a little button— it rang a bell in the kitchen, which was just off the side at the other end of the table. That would summon "the help."

At dinner, the grown-ups began their wonderful stories. We considered certain rumored behaviors of some folks about town. We laughed at events of the past week. And the guest-of-honor was a friend of mine— now a good old-fashioned Southern fried chicken.

CHAPTER EIGHT

I SPENT LONG STRETCHES IN ELIZABETHTOWN, especially during the war years when my father was away from home. My sister had not yet been born. She would be a real "baby boomer." When my father was at home, he and my mother and I would stay at our apartment in Richmond, and there he bequeathed to me two great gifts.

The first that I recall was a sense of history interlocked with a distinctly Southern sense of place. All around us, history was palpable. Just a few yards away loomed the statue of General Thomas J. "Stonewall" Jackson mounted on his horse and facing north. Years later when I learned that General P.G.T. Beauregard had remarked at the Battle of Bull Run: "And there stands Jackson like a stone wall," I could relate. The statue radiates that impression.

He's still standing there, and I pass by often. Sometimes I even salute, mimicking the eminent biographer of Robert E. Lee, the late Dr. Douglas Southall Freeman, who, on his way to work at The Richmond News Leader, would salute as he passed General Lee's south-facing statue a few blocks to the east.

On many of the plentiful sunny warm days, the neighborhood moms would take us little ones a few blocks away to the spacious grounds behind the Virginia Museum of Fine Arts. There stood an imposing Italianate mansion, the Robinson House, named for the proprietors of the land which once made up their farm. Add a lightning-lit stormy night and the old Robinson House would have made a perfect place for our neighborhood's own Boo Radley.

After the Civil War's devastation, the Robinson House and surrounding land were bequeathed to the citizens of Virginia. The old house anchored a strip through the middle of the property which would be set aside "in perpetuity" as a Confederate Memorial Park by the Virginia General Assembly.

When I was a little boy, the Robinson House was known as the Confederate Old Soldiers Home. Although the last veteran to live there had died in 1940, sons of Confederate veterans were still there when we visited. They were often joined by other veterans still living around Richmond. At my age, though, they were all just old men who liked to sit in the shade, play checkers and watch us kids play on the grounds.

A favorite climb-able, of course, was a Napoleon cannon, the Confederacy's mainstay artillery piece. And there were cannon balls casually cast about as if the war had just ended and had yet to be ennobled in the old city's collective id, as it was sure to be.[6]

Many years later, I took my then-small children to that same place and informed them of its heritage. By then the renovated and restored Robinson House, no longer looking like a backdrop for Psycho, was used for offices and classrooms for the Virginia Museum. I told my kids— with some drama, I might add— that I had been right there when I was their ages and had actually spoken with real veterans of the Civil War. The look that I got was priceless— the credulous look of the innocent which nevertheless conveyed a look of dreadful accusation: "you must be really, really old."

Those were great days for me. They and my earlier history lessons still instruct me up to the very present.

The second great lesson from my father came during the war when he was at home and we would get out the maps. I sat with him at an old library table in our living room as many an evening we listened to the radio news of Allied progress in the Battle of Europe following the D-Day invasion.

My father loved to draw, and I watched as he made meticulous notations on

National Geographic maps of Occupied Europe as the war effort progressed. He drew lines that showed where the Nazi and Allied forces were engaged. I recall my anxiety as those lines ebbed and flowed. I lived it, felt the tension, and all was reified by the resonant voices of H. V. Kaltenborn, Lowell Thomas and Edward R. Morrow "speaking from London" as we listened to the radio. They spoke with confident urgency and sonorous assuredness of "our boys" and their momentous strivings and sacrifices. And my father continued his pencil markings day-by-day across the face of France and into Belgium and finally across the Rhine and into Germany and Victory in Europe.

By the time I got to school, the war was over, and my sister had joined the family. Life was new. I was learning then, for sure, perhaps more outside the school's curriculum than within.

What was most important for me was not school. That was routine. Sure, we had good neighborhood schools and I made many friends there and learned much over the years, but there was always a sort-of mediocrity to it, a play to the lowest common denominator where creative thought was suspect. That was my feeling anyway about the public schools I attended. For example, one moment has always stood out in my memory:

When I was in the 7th grade, the last grade of elementary school in that day, with high school being grades 8 through 12, one of our study-areas was geography.

I had been immersed in geography since I was a toddler. I had walked Civil War battlefields and studied their maps. So if there was one thing I knew a little bit about, it was geography and what maps told us.

My maternal grandfather had had the foresight to subscribe to the National Geographic magazine, and for years I had access to issues dating from the 30s to the present day. It is still a tradition carried out by my own son today. He even has all of them– going back to the great magazine's beginning– on a CD.

Growing up I read all of the issues– they had been saved in a built-in bookcase behind my grandmother's baby grand piano. I marveled each time the Geographic published one of its maps and I glommed it up and compared it with what I saw on my father's globe of the world.

So when my 7th Grade teacher one day asked my somnolent class— trying to focus on a big map of Alaska, wishing we were there, the open windows testifying to the Virginia heat and humidity in those pre-AC days— "Who can tell me where the panhandle of Alaska is?"— it was I whose hand popped up immediately. "It's here," said I, pointing to the narrow part of Alaska that juts southward along the Pacific coast beside the Canadian Province of British Columbia.

"How do you know?" she asked.

"Because it looks like the handle of a pan," said I, adding, perhaps gratuitously, ...or maybe the handle of a pot, actually."

I was dismissed with a curt: "Does anyone else know where the panhandle of Alaska is?"

The silence was as sticky as the humid air, and the teacher quickly backtracked, doubtless remembering something from Elementary Education 101 that if the map did not say specifically, we might not have the good sense to figure it out for ourselves— government schools' clay feet. Was that the "lesson" of this experience? That if it didn't say so on the map, it didn't exist? It was not for me.

And that was when things I had heard among grownups became clear: that just because someone says something is true, it might not be. I began to learn to think critically, an attribute that would soon both desert me and serve me well.

High school became a time of real discovery. All of a sudden, school became important and relevant. I learned how to really write, and I could write in an environment where it was not just required but encouraged. I continued to learn outside of school too. Only then it bore the imprimatur of "extra-curricular activity," a good thing, blessed by the powers that were because it would help their college acceptance rate (and mine too). Nothing like a little bureaucratic self-interest to tap into when needed.

First it was the theater. I feared speaking before groups, so when a friend and I saw in the 'paper a call for auditions by none other than the Virginia Museum Theater for its upcoming production of *Our Town*– we went. I figured it would help me overcome my fear of audiences, and it did. In fact, I discovered I could be even a bit of a ham.

The Museum Theater[7] was looking for high school kids to work backstage, as well as try out for some roles for young people. My friend and I landed roles as the two paperboys in Thornton Wilder's classic take on life in Grover's Corners, New Hampshire.

We got to work backstage too, and *Our Town* was the beginning of several plays during the late 50s that I participated in. It was a terrific experience. One in particular stands out.

During a production of George Bernard Shaw's *Major Barbara*, my role was backstage helper. Because of a total scene-change mid-act, an entire set backdrop was lifted out of the audience's sight at the same time a new one dropped into place– all with the curtain open. A bit edgy, I understood, and only effective if the timing was perfect.

Because the large counterweights involved in moving full-stage backdrops up and down could collide with the steel catwalk seventy feet above stage, making loud clanging sounds, I and a colleague were assigned the job of waiting out the entire act on the catwalk. When the weights came upwards towards the catwalk as the new set dropped to the stage, our jobs were to hold the counterweights' cables out from the catwalk. That would prevent the weights from clanging against the steel catwalk. Simple... unless you're a teenager.

Night after night through endless rehearsals, we trudged up the spiral staircase at the back of the stage to the catwalk. We took up our positions to wait for the weights to zoom up through the gloom below. The weights would appear suddenly because of the dimmed lighting just off Stage Right. But after so many rehearsals, to sit on a catwalk through an entire act of a play we had practically memorized became boring. And boring for teenagers is especially risky.

One night, we decided to take some snacks up with us. The night happened to be special. In fact, it was a major event. It marked the beginning of the show's run: an exclusive showing, closed to the general public.

The house was filled with dignitaries. Since the VMT was part of the Virginia Museum of Fine Arts, it was a state agency. "Opening Night" was reserved for the Governor, a variety of senior state officials, major donors and benefactors of the Museum, and families of the theater company. Backstage that night, all of us in the company– from stage hands to the lead performers– were wired, especially the stickler of a stage manager whose punctilious presence seemed everywhere at once, declaring: "Nothing Must Go Wrong," and looking for anything that could be out of place.

He missed our Nabs and bottled Cokes as we hustled up the plain metal spiral stairway to the catwalk. The show went on, and finally, up came the counterweights. They caught us off guard. We jumped up, reached our posts and began to alter the courses of the massive iron weights– but not the trajectory of one of the Coke bottles which one of us had kicked in our panic to get in place in time. Off the bottle flew into the void. Its arc had it headed straight to Center Stage. But it took forever. Time was reduced to extreme slow-motion. We were transfixed with fear, awe and apocalyptic anticipation.

Horrified, we watched as every light in the house glinted off the sculpted, translucent sea-island green Coke bottle as it descended, gracefully rolling and perfectly timed to crash onto the stage just as the leading lady emoted her first lines of the new scene.

True troopers they were on that stage that night, though. The pros know that the worst thing to do in a situation like that is nothing. The bottle shattered near mid-stage, and instantly the lead actor ad-libbed around the rather rude interruption of a Coca-Cola bottle from nowhere crashing on the floor of a Victorian parlor. I do not remember it exactly, but I'm sure it was something like this:

> *Ye gads! There it is again. Bloody stupid help botched the candelabra covers once more... and in such an ugly shade of puce, too. One would think they'd have learned something working here, wot?...*

When the act was over, the curtain down, and the house lights up, the stage manager materialized at the foot of the circular stairs leading up to our steel aerie, his perfectionistic glower mimicking Iago leering at Othello, his face a florid match for his wavy red hair.

We were chewed out pretty good, but got to carry on anyway– couldn't fire volunteers, I guess– but with all snacks banned forever from anywhere near the stage, backstage, the green room, control panels, in fact *anywhere* if you were under eighteen.

CHAPTER NINE

JUSTLY CHASTISED AND NOW AT LEAST a small notch closer to adulthood, my self-education now took on a techie tinge. I cranked up my interest in amateur radio. When I was a Boy Scout, I earned the Scout's "Radio" Merit Badge. In the process I learned to copy Morse Code on short-wave radio and enough radio theory to pass the Federal Communications Commission's test to become licensed as a "ham" of a different kind.

By the time I was a sophomore in high school, I had become a part of a group of fifteen or so guys who also were amateur radio operators, and we were all on the air. We were the "geeks" of our day. We'd talk all day at school about our hobby, and then rush home after school— with allowances made for the part-time jobs I and most others had to support our adventures— and talk some more to each other on our shortwave "rigs." That's why today's teens' incessant texting and Tweeting don't bother me. I understand teenagers will communicate prolifically and use all media at their disposal. I did, too.

The FCC issued me the call letters K4GLX, and I'm still licensed today, although I am largely inactive because of life's many other callings. But I recall well and fondly the excitement and wonder of working a radio transmitter and receiver to contact hams all over the world. I logged contacts with them throughout Europe— even one behind the Iron Curtain in Czechoslovakia— as well as Canada, Mexico and most states in the U.S. That hobby soon led me to yet another great adventure of life (once more, outside of school).

One of the men in my church was director of Buildings and Grounds for the fast-growing Medical College of Virginia campus in downtown Richmond. He asked me and one of my ham buddies if we'd be interested in a project for the summer. Because it was the 1950s and state governments did not spend money like drunken sailors, as they do today, his office had gone to the Norfolk Naval Base and acquired the intercom system from a ship that was being decommissioned. It consisted of an amplifier and a hundred or so three-and-a-half-inch speakers. Because of our experience with electronics, he worked with us to come up with a way to wire those speakers up behind every other seat in an amphitheater-style lecture room at the medical college– one where surgeons would perform operations under the lights and at the same time describe what they were doing to the students seated in the mini-stadium of a classroom.

We did. It worked. And that led me to a job the following summer at MCV– again in Buildings and Grounds. I had just graduated from high school, and the experience was to be a major milestone in my life-long pursuit of the liberal arts.

I worked in a little office on the bottom floor of McGuire Hall, a major teaching building scaled to complement the neighborhood of historic nineteenth century homes, including the residence of Jefferson Davis, a building known as the White House of the Confederacy.

My boss that summer was an Englishman named Robbins who counted on me to maintain some of the basic functions in the building and help out other staff as needs arose. The official crematorium for the Commonwealth of Virginia was just next door in a secure part of the building. A cheerful and affable black man named Boaz managed the crematorium. It was not long before we became friends. When things were not too busy, we would sit in the alley behind the crematorium and autopsy the world's problems. Then one day after I had established myself as a part of the team, I suppose, and with the assent of my boss, Boaz asked me if I would help him out occasionally with his job. Recognizing a golden opportunity to broaden my world-view, and bursting with curiosity, I quickly agreed. I became a sort-of part-time de-facto crematorium factotum.

The crematorium existed to dispose of the remains of research animals, certain medical detritus and even human bodies, bodies of people who died unclaimed in state institutions like hospitals, asylums and prisons. It was used also to dispose of bodies that were found and unclaimed after a statutorily required period of time. These would have included vagrants and crime victims, for example.

One day several State Police cars and two ambulances arrived in the discreet alleyway behind the anonymous loading dock of the crematorium. State Police officers sealed off the alley, and I knew something big was up. I didn't say a word. But I watched.

The bodies from an apparent murder-suicide had been discovered in an abandoned Cadillac on remote farmland deep in the Virginia countryside several months after the deed had been done. They were found sealed up in the car on a steamy, hot summer day. As the law required, they were brought to Richmond for disposal. Their remains were in rubber body-bags. Their removal from the ambulances, surrounded by grim-faced State Troopers backed up by a sizeable contingent of Richmond City Police officers keeping people away from the area, marked my first direct insight into life's dark side. You can hide from reality, but it will always catch up with you.

As if that weren't enough for one day, later that morning, my moment of full initiation to the cryptic and sometimes creepy intrigues of a major medical college had not yet come, but was imminent.

Across the hall from my spot was a lab where a doctor conducted research. His assistants were a pair of third-year medical students. Friendly fellows they were... and eager to initiate me, the kid, into the esoterica of a major teaching hospital. I knew it was coming. After all, the depths of a medical teaching building hold weird things most people never see or imagine– things like rooms full of animals slit open on their backs with tubes of ominous liquids flowing in and out of them– tubes connected to machines that hummed a Mussorgsky dirge.

The crematorium was another example, as was the Vat Room, which was up a ramp and into a stark chamber next to the crematorium. The Vat Room was where cadavers were stored. There were dozens of them. They were on hangers, immersed two deep in huge vats filled with some kind of strong-smelling preservative chemical. When a class needed cadavers, an electronic hoist pulled the double-hung rows of naked dead people up and clear of the vats. The display was like a scene in Robin Cook's Coma, and my adolescent mind could have turned the Vat Room into a zombie incubator in the bat of an eye.

I had seen all this, of course, by the time my "initiation" neared that morning. But I could not imagine how my med-student buddies across the hall could top any of it. They tried, however.

The morning was routine. I checked our supply inventory. I discussed the day with Mr. Robbins. I flirted with the pretty nurse down the hall. All was right with the world of medical science, yet I sensed a subtle boding.

It was not long before my med student buddies strolled across the hall with quirky grins on their faces. I knew this was it, the Initiation Rite. But I was ready, Boy Scout training in full "Be Prepared" mode. And I knew they couldn't fool K4GLX. I had done Morse Code on short-wave radio with Communists, after all.

They asked me to go to room three-hundred and something and recharge the fire extinguisher. It had been used to put out a brief, small fire earlier, they said.
"Sure," said I, "be back shortly, and then you guys can tell me what happened with the State Police and all."

Their glee was all too transparent. But I got my fire-extinguisher stuff and rolled.

First clue: The name on the double doors to the large medical classroom read "Gross Anatomy Lab."

Undaunted, I pushed through both doors like Gary Cooper into the High Noon Saloon.

Instantly I was in another world. Arrayed before me on table after table lay shallow black trays like I remembered from my high school biology class. But instead of earthworms, the trays held hands, human hands, splayed out as if in protest. They should have been, for they were being dismantled in a process known as dissection. That's a nice term for what lay before me: Skin slit and pulled back revealed layers of muscles, tendons, veins and bones, all immersed in more of that sinister chemical I had smelled in the Vat Room. It was formaldehyde, a familiar odor to me by then.

That scene was a surprise but nothing like confronting the zombie incubator downstairs, or seeing what dead people looked like through the tiny window of a crematorium when the gas jets were fired.

What a letdown. Surely those guys were capable of better than that. I was totally unimpressed. Earthworms and frogs were grosser. But then, as I walked into the room looking for the fire extinguisher, the smell of formaldehyde became stronger than it should have been.

It dawned on me that the display of hands was a ruse, a sneaky diversion to put me at ease. The fire extinguisher was on the far wall, where it was supposed to be. But the room was "L" shaped. The test would be around the corner of the "L."

I had not turned on the overhead fluorescent lights when I entered. So with just the ambience of an overcast day outside casting a grim pall over the whole scene, I began a cautious walk to the end of the room. Around the corner to my right, I spotted the gurney first.

Then the body.

There was a cadaver on the gurney with no cover, just a gray, dead human lying there.

So this was the test. I went over to have a close look. It was going to be a long summer, after all, and who knew what might come next if I failed this test? I made myself touch the cadaver. Cadavers feel rubbery and flatulent, like a partly deflated beach ball. No big deal.

Then, knowing myself to have passed the test, objective Doug kicked in: This is a laboratory specimen for scientific study, I told myself. Leonardo daVinci himself chopped these things into pieces and sketched them without a moment's hesitation. Then he went and painted The Last Supper. So go recharge the fire extinguisher and have lunch, Doug.

I did. Have lunch, that is. The fire extinguisher did not need recharging. It had never been used, its original seal was unbroken, so the test was a setup. The guys were doubtless expecting me to return pale and retching. Instead, I ate my lunch in serenity outside under a tree. Grinning to myself, I tried to imagine how the great daVinci would have handled this scene.

I trust that Twenty-first Century readers will understand that much of what I am relating would not be likely– or even legal– under the burden of federal and state laws and regulations that we are subject to today as we hurtle hell-bent-for-leather into the Nanny State.

No, these were the Ozzie and Harriet days, the times of huge fins on cars with enormous V-8 engines that got maybe ten miles per twenty-five-cent gallon of gas. Everybody had guns. Many adults smoked cigarettes– "More Doctors Smoke Camels Than Any Other Cigarette," read one magazine ad of the times. Men wore suits and fedoras, and women dressed up to shop, and white gloves were not at all out of place downtown.

But the times, they were a'changin'.

Maybe it's been the unprecedented prosperity we've enjoyed relative to the rest of the world, while whole swaths of our own cities languish in poverty. Or could it have been the curse of "political correctness" that doesn't promote– even denies– honest discourse among humans?

Then came 1968. For me, that year was the fulcrum of those times. Robert Kennedy and Martin Luther King were assassinated. Vietnam was being lost to bureaucratic and political micro-management by men who had never served. A president who was a shoo-in for reelection quit. Whole cityscapes burned. I was moving inexorably towards my alcoholic crash. That awful year did not help, but I was maintaining appearances and a reasonable facsimile of stable family life.

By then, I was a young working family man. My daughter had been born earlier that year. Many days I rode the bus downtown to my PR job with the power company. When I stepped off my bus one morning at Eighth and Broad Streets in downtown Richmond, I found myself face-to-face with armed soldiers.

The Virginia Army National Guard had been activated and was stationed throughout downtown. Rioters had set Washington on fire, just a hundred miles away. Richmond could have been next. Two soldiers were stationed on each downtown corner, and I'll never forget my sadness upon seeing that. My country, city, and state were beset by some unnamed upheaval. I felt fear for my family, and my deep sense of history told me yet another era was going away with the wind. And would tomorrow be another day?

As an active Army Reservist, we trained on weekends for urban riot control. The training was realistic: burning buildings, tear gas randomly thrown into the mix, the noise of explosions— all with two groups facing off. One unit would be rioters, the other soldiers trying to control and push back the rioters.

For some reason we were never called to that duty. I was grateful, for the thought of facing my fellow citizens with an M-14 rifle with bayonet affixed, was almost too much. Why did I think that way? I had a job, a house in the suburbs and a good education. Why not be content and grateful for just that? And angry with the malcontents who just seemed bent on burning, looting, and lawlessness?

The answer lay beneath the veneer of urban cowboy I had become, just below the placid outside that I hid from a turbulent inside with liberal doses of alcohol most every day. That answer was entombed in extensive self-deception. It lay deep within my conscience, where I questioned, denied and debated with myself, but which I would later recall and understand— the conscience my mother had inspired in me.

CHAPTER TEN

MY MOTHER WAS A REMARKABLE PERSON. She was an accomplished pianist, a lover of all kinds of music, especially classical and the swing-era classics of Glenn Miller, Tommy Dorsey, Duke Ellington and many others. As a child and perhaps as counterpoint to that earlier war– the one we were all engaged in fighting– I absorbed the love of good music.

The memory of seeing my mother at home in North Carolina, dressed in her summer "frock," as her mother called dresses in those steamy sticky days, sitting on the bench of the Steinway baby grand piano and playing Beethoven's Moonlight Sonata in the late-afternoon quiet on the river hill, is still with me. To this day I hear the mellifluous chords, feel the serenity and catch the scent of fresh-cut chrysanthemums embellishing the classical décor overseen by a formal oil painting of my great-grandfather– mustachioed, bald and stern of visage.

Years later, my own hair line rapidly receding– I have the bald gene– I grew a mustache so I could look more like my great-grandfather, a Confederate veteran, who had enlisted as a teenager towards the end. A horseman from youth, he became a "junior ranger," a teenagers' cavalry auxiliary, in General Joe Johnston's last-gasp effort to link up with Lee in the spring of 1865. That long-shot liaison was not to be. Lee surrendered the Army of Northern Virginia at Appomattox on April 9, and on April 17 Johnston surrendered to General William Tecumseh Sherman near Durham Station, North Carolina. My great-grandfather's war was over.

He was paroled by a generous Union and went on to a reasonably successful life that ended in 1932. But that classic portrait, embellished by my mother's and my grandmother's recollections, made him one of my early heroes, and I think my mother inherited much of his spirit (but not the bald gene) from what I understood after watching and listening to my families' stories over the years.

My mother took me to school for my first day in the third grade. The sturdy old school building sat amongst a grove of huge oak trees. Their shade, the building's thick solid walls, high ceilings and tall open windows comprised what passed of air conditioning in those days. Indoors it was pleasant, but in the midst of the usual controlled chaos of the first day of school, there were two quiet twin boys who did not have enough lunch money or the pencils and other things required for our class.

My mother noticed, though, along with the absence of the boys' parents. She went and got them the accoutrements of scholarly occupation they required and gave them lunch money.

I remember that most vividly, a quiet act of kindness.

Many years later, when my son and I were about to embark on one of our adventures, a trip to hike in Virginia's Blue Ridge Mountains, we stopped in a 7-11 for Twinkies, coffee for me and hot chocolate for him – and plenty of spring water.

We planned a rigorous 9.2-mile hike of a challenging mountain called The Priest in Nelson County. The tallest mountain in the area, The Priest stands majestically astride the Appalachian Trail. Along with water, we stashed lots of trail-mix bars to go along with the sandwiches we had fixed. Thus provisioned, we went back to the car. I realized the clerk had returned to me a dollar and some change too much. Even though we were anxious to go, I told my son to wait, as I went to give it back to the young clerk. Then we rolled, and I thought no more about it.

However, years later my son replayed that episode to me as one of the lessons of his upbringing that made him careful about not ever deliberately cheating anyone.

Little things? I think not. Two seemingly small events– lunch money, pencils, and paper for those boys and returned change for a store deal– but they had grown into much more.

∽ ⊶ ⊷ ∾

Many years later my mother, by then widowed and living alone, bequeathed to me a kind-of dénouement to her earlier instruction to me on race relations, "the rest of the story," as Paul Harvey would have said.

As a youngster growing up during the turbulent 50s and 60s– times of racial unrest, as the old South's death-grip on a segregated society was finally being pried loose– my mother taught me in no uncertain terms that black folks, as God's creations, were coequal in God's eyes with all other people. So segregation was wrong, she taught me, and Negroes deserved full admission into society. That meant no more sitting in the back of the bus. No more second-rate seats in movie theaters. No more of the patronizing charade of "separate-but-equal" schools.

The legacy she left me has served me well, and it proved its punch years later one day, when in her waning years, she told me one of those startling things that sometimes just pop forth from ones parents as they age.

By then she was well into her seventies, still living in the same house she and my father had bought in 1949, and in which my sister and I had grown up. Dad had died, and even though my mother had many friends nearby, I still checked by the house from time to time to see how things were going.

One day I happened by in the midst of "March Madness," the Atlantic Coast Conference basketball championships, followed by the NCAA national basketball tournament, which seemed always to feature her favorite team, the University of North Carolina Tarheels.

The old house was small, but it had a warmth to it that was always ours. She sat on the sofa in the living room. On the wall behind were her three treasured prints of colorful indigenous birds, to the side were her two large hand-made bookcases.

75

Bookcases that held the geneses of my own love of books. The bookcases had been a work of love themselves, made by Vander, a big gentle black man who had worked in my mother's family for years. Vander made them as a wedding present for my mother.

But March Madness was not a time of either book-reading or bird-watching, for my mom's eyes were riveted on an old eighteen-inch television screen as the ACC took on the titans of the Big Ten, Big East, Southeastern conferences and others. Fortunately for Carolina, the legendary Coach Dean Smith was at his peak and those were the years of Michael Jordan's ascendancy. Without question, Jordan was her favorite player of all time. The reason for that is that Mr. Jordan hailed from Wilmington, North Carolina, forty miles from where my mother grew up. He was a homie.

While I understood– and shared– her Tarheel loyalty, her love of basketball was outsized for a woman her age. So, on that visit curiosity got the best of me:

"Momma," I said, as the little television set cut to a commercial, "how'd you get so interested in basketball?"

With a sort-of what-kind-of-dumb-question-is-that look– one that mirrored the spirit of the rather cheeky beer ad on the tube– she replied, "because I used to play it."

"But where did you play?" I asked.

Elizabethtown was a small town. I had trouble remembering where there were any basketball courts at all, except perhaps in the high school gym.

"Did Elizabethtown High School have a girls' basketball team?" I asked, thinking to myself how unusual that would have been in the 20s and 30s in the South.

"Not officially," she said with a hint of Scarlett O'Hara's defiance in her eyes," Teenage girls were expected to be 'Southern ladies,'" she said with a pert smirk of irony, "and playing basketball my way didn't work with that."

"Your way? What was that?"

Again with that look– one that said "surely we've been over this before"– she laid this bombshell on me:

"I would put on my basketball stuff, sneak out of the house through the back door, go through the neighbors' backyards across the railroad tracks to 'New Town' and play basketball with the black boys."

At this revelation, I know my expression must have reflected jaw-dropping amazement.

Catching my vibe, she explained: "They became my friends. They recognized that I could play basketball just about as well as some of them. So I was accepted as just another one of the boys," she said. "And it was great. We had a good time, and we'd play basketball. That's how I learned how it actually worked on the court, and that's why I know what's really happening on TV. So that's why I watch."

"Did you ever get caught?" asked I– because as the teenage daughter of a well-positioned white family playing basketball with "the boys" in a small Southern town certainly would have been viewed askance by some in those days of calcified attitudes, Jim Crow laws, and segregated schools.

Also, I knew my grandmother– a serious daughter of the old South who had grown up in Georgia with fresh memories of Sherman's March– would have had what they used to call a "conniption fit," if she found out.

As it turned out, of course, she did– fit and all.

"So what did she say once she found out?" I asked, bug-eyed and grateful the TV station had just gone local to some kind of dopey used car "sales extravaganza."

"She told me never to do that again," she deadpanned through the edges of another one of those smirks, this one with a twinkle in her eye.

"It is just something you simply do not do," she said, mimicking my grandmother's genteel manner while skillfully skirting the conniption part. "And your father would have more heart trouble than he's already got if he were to find out," she added.

"But you kept going, I'll bet."

"Of course," she said, and the coverage returned to live action." It's a long time ago, but I loved playing basketball, and now I love watching it."

I was amazed. But not particularly surprised. I think I would have done the same thing myself, under the circumstances. Nevertheless, the story's one of the most object lessons of life my mother ever gave me all those years ago.

My father imparted not only indelible memories of the grandeur of history and the momentous consequences of things half a world away, but lessons that would last long after his earthly life.

His hallmark was precision. He was an accountant, wore a green eye shade and used garters to hold up the sleeves of his starched, white business shirt. When I went to his office downtown— a modest building across the street from the newspapers' block-long printing press building— I noticed they all dressed like that, all the accountants. And they all cranked away at large mechanical calculators that generated yards of narrow paper rolls. They fell to the floor behind the desks. I collected the ones they didn't need. You could make some neat stuff with them.

Besides being an accountant, my dad was a Boy Scout leader. I was later to call him the oldest Boy Scout I ever knew. In nearly sixty years of service to that honorable organization, he earned the coveted Silver Beaver Award to accompany his earlier induction into the Order of the Arrow— two of scouting's highest honors.

He died in 1989. Seven years later, I had left my car for service in a garage near where I grew up, and the overweight, somewhat rumpled man with a troubled face behind the counter looked at me with a light in his eye that had not been there before he read my name on the service ticket.

"Was your father Mr. Blue with Troop 660?" he asked quietly. [8]

"Yes," I said. "He sure was."

Then the most touching thing happened. This man, a little younger than I and one, I sensed, who had seen trouble in life, teared up as he recalled his time with that Boy Scout troop— and the skills of being a good Scout and a good man he had learned from my dad and the other leaders. That's a moment I'll never forget, a message from a worldly life ended but with a light that still shined.

PART THREE

Secrets and the Mirror

CHAPTER ELEVEN

HOW WAS IT, THEN, WITH SUCH A BENEFICENT upbringing and a life's course so hopeful, that I would come to cry out "Why me?" when alcoholism reared its ugly head as I lost the path that does not stray?

I began to think I was crazy sometime near the end of 1973. The Luger's image still hung like a dark medieval tapestry, while the creepy-strange mirror awaited its time, covert in the underworld of my mind.

If there is reason in crazy, it is that nothing in my upbringing or world-view warned me that things would come to this.

But neither was I a naïf traipsing through life in my own little world. I had been raised well but not unduly sheltered. I knew there were people with alcohol problems. I saw the grown-ups in my family and their friends drink on many occasions, and a few drunk at times.

After all, folks seemed happier with alcohol– maybe even healthier. We used it medicinally sometimes. My mother had an awful-tasting concoction of honey and bourbon for sore throats in the winter. And there were sporting uses: when the men went out to hunt, alcohol went too. It would keep you warm in a duck blind on a frigid pond.

So no. Those early views did not answer the question. I saw alcohol as a social lubricant, an aid to digestion, a medicine, a relaxant, and a celebratory must. Never once did I suspect that it could be an addictive killer.

One day not long ago, a close acquaintance was well on her way to inebriation when she walked into her dining room, faltered, took on a look of absolute fear and fell dead. Before she died, she must have known she was falling into her own blood.

The medical term was "exsanguination," they told me. The witness, another close acquaintance, saw it as a veritable explosion of blood out of her mouth as she fell. My friend had drunk for many years, and didn't skip a beat after the baleful day physicians told her she had to stop. She had cirrhosis of the liver. To continue to drink would kill her, the doctors said. She did, and it did. She drank herself to death. Her aorta, which carried blood pumped from the heart with enough force to send it coursing throughout the body, was weakened by the disease and alcohol's assault. It burst as she breathed her last.

Suicide by another name? Perhaps. But I'm afraid that it was not that simple. I'm afraid— just as I've seen several friends continue to smoke cigarettes after diagnoses of lung cancer or emphysema— that her death was not a deliberate act of suicide but a perfect example of the insanity of addiction.

It's probably not medically correct, but some say insanity is continuing to repeat negative behavior, expecting different results each time. Surely this avoidable tragedy was one of those all-too-human failings that tell us: "But it won't happen to me."

I learned that lesson early in sobriety, and this experience was too close for comfort. It rivets my gratitude to have been spared thus far. But still my querulousness at what I was soon to experience loomed.

Alcoholism and alcohol abuse are part of the human condition. They have marched alongside people throughout history. Ten thousand years ago, Mesopotamians figured out how to make bread with barley. In the process, they discovered beer. The Sumerians served up beer and wine 6,000 years ago at a busy trading post called Godin Tepe, an area of modern-day Iran. In 330 BC Alexander the Great led his armies against Persopolis while under the influence of alcohol. And Genghis Khan ordered his soldiers "not to get drunk often... or more than once a week."

According to Donald W. Goodwin's book *Alcoholism: the Facts*, "One of the myths of our times is that the stresses of modern living have produced a society unusually reliant on alcohol. This is not true. Per-capita consumption in the USA was highest at an estimated six or seven gallons per person in the early 1800s when wine and cider were the favorite beverages."[9]

So my "Why Me" grousing had nothing to do with some supercilious modern-day conceit that our "fast-paced" digital world is blowing some folks off the tracks and under the bridge. The problem has always been a characteristic of the unchanging fallibility inherent in the human condition, perhaps genetic, certainly another cross to bear.

As for me– after drinking up all the superciliousness I could lay my hands on– I knew "Why Me?" was the wrong question. The right one was: "What do you do about it?"

"Why?" was in the ballpark with handwringing hysteria. Of course it was egocentric and beyond the pale of the unexamined life. My question about what to do about a serious alcohol problem, one getting perilously close to health consequences, was about to be answered as 1973 drew to a portentous close.

CHAPTER TWELVE

THE ACCEPTED DEFINITION OF ALCOHOLISM has wobbled over the years. One of the first to really nail it was none other than Dr. Benjamin Rush, the Revolutionary War-era polymath who, in 1784, was the first to call alcoholism a "disease."[10] Its modern definition is found in the Fourth Edition of the Diagnostic and Statistical Manual, the bible of mental health practitioners:

A maladaptive pattern of alcohol use, leading to clinically significant impairment or distress, as manifested by three or more of the following seven criteria, occurring at any time in the same 12-month period:

1. *Tolerance, as defined by either of the following:*

   a) A need for markedly increased amounts of alcohol to achieve intoxication or desired effect.

   b) Markedly diminished effect with continued use of the same amount of alcohol.

2. *Withdrawal, as defined by either of the following:*

   a) The characteristic withdrawal syndrome for alcohol (refer to DSM-IV for further details).

   b) Alcohol is taken to relieve or avoid withdrawal symptoms.

3. *Alcohol is often taken in larger amounts or over a longer period than was intended.*

4. *There is a persistent desire or there are unsuccessful efforts to cut down or control alcohol use.*

5. *A great deal of time is spent in activities necessary to obtain alcohol, use alcohol or recover from its effects.*

6. *Important social, occupational, or recreational activities are given up or reduced because of alcohol use.*

7. *Alcohol use is continued despite knowledge of having a persistent or recurrent physical or psychological problem that is likely to have been caused or exacerbated by the alcohol (e.g., continued drinking despite recognition that an ulcer was made worse by alcohol consumption).* [11]

Many other definitions exist, of course, probably just as many as there are people who've ever experienced alcohol abuse or had close relatives who have. Even Abraham Lincoln had something to say about such "intemperance:"

"I have not inquired at what period of time the use of intoxicating liquors commenced; nor is it important to know. It is sufficient that, to all of us who now inhabit the world, the practice of drinking then is just as old as the world itself— that is, we have seen the one just as long as we have seen the other. [12]

The DSM's definition, especially phrases like "A maladaptive pattern of alcohol use" appealed to me, the old me, the me who searched for complexity and intellectual solutions, of Platonic self-examination, all while still trudging through the Bottom. I learned the hard way that intellectualizing about drinking is an artful dodge. Relying on Plato to sober up is a zero-sum gambit, not to mention foolish self-deception. Nothing will ever come of it save another snort. A 'maladaptive pattern' of anything will send me to the dictionary, not Lincolnian truth, and very possibly a misstep into that bottom of quicksand with its relentless, sucking, slow suffocation.

The short version of my working definition of alcoholism is that emotion got in front of rationality and intellect, and emotion won. E/I=Trouble.

I grew up seeing adults in the family experience good times with their friends, lubricated by alcohol. So my emotions registered a plus, a desire to do the same once I grew up. As I moved along I saw similar signals in the culture: movies, music, ads and their one-sided portrayals of beer- and whiskey-drinking, much of it with sexual innuendo. My takeaway was that drinking transformed life by making it all seem better, in fact just great with no possible downside.

But for an alcoholic there is a progression, one that can fool the best of us, because in the beginning all seems well— even normal, if there is such a thing. What we do not know when the progression started is that we had been propagandized by a culture of denial. And once we left for college or got our first job out of high school, we were free to do those grownup things. So we did.

Most can handle them, of course, but a percentage of our population cannot. If we are in that percentage, if we drew that card, then one day we will tip over into true addiction. Then it gets back to feelings. If a physician says to one of us, "You need to cut back on your drinking," the emotional formula works itself out to its logical conclusion: Trouble. That's the way it was for me although I recognize that there are many paths to addiction, some beginning at very young ages and others triggered by unspeakable abuse. I was spared that but I learned how to always rationalize drinking. Then the next one. And the next. And I'm hooked. On what could be a one-way street.

As I looked at my own addiction, an analog was cars. That fixation's legacy would soon lead to trouble.

As a teenager, I read *Road & Track* magazine. The adventure and romance of European road racing fascinated me. I could imagine Count Wolfgang von Trips roaring around *Der Nürburgbing*. Or Phil Hill, Stirling Moss, Ludovico Scarfiotti, Lorenzo Bandini— all heroes to me— racing like the wind on curvy civilian streets or tracks like Le Mans. I thrilled when I learned that the Ford GT 40 actually had a wing— one that would force the car tires downward onto the pavement at speeds in excess of 140 miles per hour, lest the car go airborne. However, what really impressed me at the time was an interview I read in a motorsports magazine with von Trips in which he admitted that knocking back a couple of German brews before a race made him a better racer.

Right away I resolved to become a better driver the same way. The disease I brought forward into adulthood was thus also propagandized by the beliefs of an adolescent whose self-constructed mechanisms of unreal glories became aspirations. No surprise then that this "better driver" accumulated a series of traffic citations climaxing with a DUI, a night in the pokie, a conviction, and– after appeal– a reduction to reckless driving, which just barely saved my privilege to drive in Virginia.

The pokie, of course, was a milestone in my saga, and it helped push me to the conclusion that I was going crazy. That, along with losing the best job I had ever had, at least in terms of money, added to the crazy feelings. But strangely those experiences worked out to be the catalysts which brought me to my senses and led to the rather frightening roller-coaster ride to actual recovery– recovery that has now lasted nearly forty years.

I was in the bottom, and I did what I had to do. At the time, my pokie-going had been very limited. I had never actually been *in* one. My wife, who had already started talking to me about separating, had taken the kids and gone to her mother's summer place on the river. I was left in the dangerous position of having too much time on my hands. I went to commiserate with a lady friend. She lived in a smaller city a few miles south of my home.

My friend and I did not do anything other than talk and drink beer. We drank alike, and drinking and talking were about it, after a certain point. But before I knew it, it was 3:30 a.m. I had about a thirty-five minute drive home, even in the best of circumstances. So I left, made my way to the main drag through town, a known speed trap, and towards the on-ramp for Interstate 95. I never made it, and I'm glad I didn't. I was in no condition to drive on the main north-south Interstate in this part of the country. But the ghost of Count von Trips was with me, now a ghost because he had died in a spectacular 200-plus-miles-per-hour crash at the Italian Grand Prix at Monza in 1961. I was pretty sure I could not make it 35 miles at 60 miles per hour.

My Formula One was a Chevy, and before I got one-hundred yards down the main street in town, headed for the Interstate, the blue flashing lights almost on my rear bumper startled me. I had no idea he was back there. I pulled off the four-lane boulevard into a shopping center's vacant parking lot. The police officer came up to my window and asked for my driver's license and automobile registration. I produced them and gave them to him, trying my best to look okay.

He was the epitome of the Southern Sheriff, a flat-brimmed "Smokey the Bear" hat aggressively canting slightly forward on his probably bald pate, a pear-shaped beer-drinkin' bubba-look about his middle. He was a dead ringer for the sheriff from *The Dukes of Hazard*, a popular TV show. The program inspired a Dodge commercial for one of its muscle cars of the day. In the ads, Joe Southern Sherriff comes up to the Luke Duke lookalike in his Dodge Charger and says in an Alabama drawl, "Lemme see your lye-sence, boy."

So naturally, when the police officer came back to see me after examining my papers in his car, I spotted his profile in my rear-view mirror, flashing blue lights silhouetting his strut, I just could not help myself. Thinking a little humor would leaven the moment, I slurred, "Say officer, you ever do any TV spots? "

"Out of the car," he growled, obviously missing my humor, "and try to stand up straight, buster, if you can!"

The officer put me through all the tests policemen do with guys in my condition: walk a straight line. Couldn't do it. Extend my arm, close my eyes and bring my index finger to my nose. Poked my left ear lobe. Recite the alphabet backwards. I got to Z. So into the back seat of his cruiser I went, handcuffed after blowing well over the legal limit into the bag, the infamous, infallible "Breathalyzer."

Arriving at the jail, I tightened up, anticipating the worst, a "drunk tank" full of psychopaths, and I was way overdressed for their company. But instead, here were three young deputies on duty in a well-lit, spotless motif. They were apparently close to their shift change and bantered with me, taking the tension out of the air, as they took my mug shot, got my finger prints and joked about my handwriting when I signed something-or-other. These guys did this all the time. There was nothing unique about me.

Then into a cell I went, fortunately by myself. I never even saw, or heard, a drunk tank. I was grateful. I dozed, then got breakfast brought to me– not bad, either. Then they processed me out, but first I had to post a bond. The bondsman showed up, only it was a bondswoman who turned out to be a classmate from high school.

Mortified– because I looked like and doubtless smelled like crap– I thought I was going to get out of there unrecognized.

I was released on bond, got my car back from the impoundment lot, and I headed home, picking up a six-pack for the trip as soon as I crossed the county line. By then it was about 8 a.m. Sunday.

CHAPTER THIRTEEN

RICHMOND'S CIVIC AUDITORIUM IS A HUGE structure on the edge of Virginia Commonwealth University's academic campus, across the street from historic Monroe Park. The structure looks like an Islamic mosque– and once was called "The Mosque"– but today, following extensive renovations, the grand structure has been renamed "Altria Theater."[13]

"Civic auditorium" is an understatement. It was developed in 1926 by the city's "ACCA Temple of the Mystic Shrine." An overwrought Shriners' meeting hall, it housed an auditorium that seated 4,000, an 18,000-square-foot ballroom and more than 24,000-square-feet of office space, all festooned with thousands of square feet of gold- and aluminum-leaf decor.

"The Mosque" failed as its original function and was sold in 1940 to the City of Richmond, which quickly turned it into a destination for symphonies, opera, travelling Broadway plays while simultaneously hosting numerous civic offices, educational centers and at one time deep in its private areas, a firing range for the police academy.

The City got itself a deal and obviously capped costs by leaving the towering minarets in place still topped with the Muslim crescent and star. Missing are Muezzins calling the Islamic faithful to prayer. Only in Richmond, I tell myself, a somewhat eccentric place of many contrasts.

It was to one of The Mosque's offices that I was referred during my meeting with my family's minister. I had called him just after the psychiatrist hung up on me and my search for the Luger proved fruitless. It was the beginning to the "What" of my odyssey. I would try pastoral counseling.

The pastor of a church I attended earlier in the 70s had told me, "You are on the road to alcoholism." But I was not ready to hear that then. Now I was, and I went to see the Rev. William Boyce. He was senior pastor of Lakeside Presbyterian Church, the church I had grown up in. Just after the dark thoughts of using the Luger to do myself in, I would find light and hope in our two-hour meeting.

"I don't think I'm that bad," I said, when he first suggested AA.

Never mind that I had lost a job, my car, and needed a haircut, but did not have enough money for one. And the impending loss of my family and house was not "that bad," either.

We sat in Bill's study, its walls lined with bookcases bearing thousands of years of history, theology, and commentary. It was collegial, calming, and a reassuring retreat. I felt myself tugged back to that time as a teenager when I would go there to read sometimes, for I was curious and open about spiritual matters.

The tenor was auspicious as Bill deftly deflected my fear of AA and directed me to an organization maintained by the City and its adjacent counties as the Division of Alcoholism Services. The DAS offices were on the Main Street side of The Mosque, a storefront entrance prominently displaying its name in big letters. Bill arranged for me to meet with a counselor there who could help me with what I agreed just might be a touch of an "alcohol problem."

My first appointment was on a bright early-June day in 1973. It felt right even before I walked in the door. The day was warm but not oppressive, newly budding flora and greenery all around– perfect outdoor beer-drinking weather, said the Mad Hatter.

There was convenient, discrete walled-in, on-site parking in the rear of the building. I had to walk from my car around the back edge of the building to the sidewalk along Main Street, a major westbound route out of the downtown business district where I had worked for most of my career.

Having been fired and now jobless, however, I feared walking eastward on Main Street the thirty or so yards to the DAS doorway, emblazoned with the big bold institutional words "Division of Alcoholism Services," because I might be– no, would be– seen by some of my old colleagues. And I could not handle that.

So at the edge of the parking lot and the building, my paranoia and I peeked around the corner and looked at the stoplight at the intersection just up the street. It was green, so traffic was flowing. I recoiled into the shadows, fearful of being spotted, while The Mad Hatter smirked in the shade.

Peeking again, I saw the light had turned red, so I scuttled around the corner and slipped into the DAS office. Reflecting months later, the epiphany of something I heard repeatedly– "alcoholism is an ego-sickness"– revealed its truth to me, and this faux-cloak-and-dagger behavior proved it.

Once inside, I felt safe. A friendly young woman greeted me. The furniture was plain government-issue wood with no color, no cushions. The wall's art was posters– things like the "12 Signs of Alcoholism" and a mysterious thing called "the Jellinek Chart." In an inverted bell curve, the chart described a progression I would soon learn all about as I saw myself plummeting down its slippery slope to "The Bottom." [14] The hallway to the counselors' offices bore drug-store-framed tenets of the AA faith: Live and Let Live, Easy Does It, One Day at a Time, Think-Think-Think, First Things First, and others.

I met with a counselor named BJ with whom I immediately felt comfortable. He asked me a series of questions, questions I was later to recognize as one of the infamous questionnaires that would reveal one's positioning along the downward slide of Dr. Jellinek's slippery slope to The Bottom. [15]

I passed the test (or failed, depending on your point of view). I qualified, shockingly close to the bottom of the downside. Then BJ surprised me with this revelation:

"I'm in recovery myself, Doug. Have been for almost five years now," BJ said.

He shared a quick overview of his drinking history and recovery, I squirmed in my un-padded wooden chair. I felt like he'd had been reading my mail, not to mention my mind, too. His story was very close to my own, I realized.

BJ looked like a semi-hippie, hair middling-long, attire office-casual before its time. This was 1974, after all, so "semi-hippie" was the day's "look" of a dying fad. But BJ's eyes bespoke the graceful attitude of one who wanted to help people like me. His eyes were very present, very much alive, not dreamy like those of the flower children of yore. Their clarity bore into my self-deceiving heart like a sailor on watch for landfall through a dense fog.

"You told me you were unemployed on the phone when you called," he said. "So what's that make home life like?"

I told him I felt like an alien there, worthless and anxious. He crossed his arms, looked into my soul and pushed and probed for more and more. I kept trying to turn the topic back to my excuses, hearing the rush of traffic on the busy street outside, wishing to go back out there.

"You know what? That worthlessness and anxiety you mentioned? That's not you. That's your disease talking to you. You have it backwards. Emotion does not win. Actions do.

"Here's something I want you to read. It tells you what we mean by calling alcoholism a disease. We believe in the disease concept here. We work with it every day, and we see success," he said. "So, what do you think it is, anyway?"

"A personal failing. I've been thinking it's a question of right and wrong."

"You really believe that?"

"Not sure anymore," I said. "But calling it a disease seems a cop-out."

"How so?"

"Like all I have to do is go to a doctor and get some pills, and it would get fixed. But, hey, I've tried that. Docs, counselors, preachers. Nothing worked."

"Counselors. I'm a counselor. What kind of counselor you talkin' about?"

He had me there. "Well, a guy who was a member of my old church. He was a probation and parole counselor for the state."

"And now, here you are. Worse off than before."

"Yeah...yeah, I need help, man. I been kidding myself. The p&p guy and I met for beers. And so did one of the preachers I talked to. Talked to me about 'cosmic thinking,'" I said, unable not to snicker at my own disconnect.

"My wife underlined articles in *Reader's Digest* like 'I Am Joe's Liver' and left them in the john for me to read. And just people, other people, are giving me the feeling that I must have gone through some kind of trouble in my childhood, but I don't really think I did."

That comment led to questions about my childhood. We agreed growing up was not bad for me. "Certainly compared with some I've seen," he said.

As we moved on, I think I began to get it. Of course my behavior had a moral side. But at the same time, it was a health problem.

"I'd rather call it a 'medical problem,'" I said. "How 'bout that?"

"Beats the hell out of beating yourself up with the crap you've been hearing, and the self-imposed moral stuff you've allowed to run your life. Look where it's gotten you.

"Drop the morality argument. You're not so special. You're just like millions of others, even people like Dick Van Dyke. You know his story?"

"Yes," I said. "I heard about that."

Van Dyke had starred in a made-for-TV movie, *The Morning After*, which had first aired on ABC-TV earlier that year. Van Dyke played the protagonist– another PR guy– who had become alcoholic. It was about that time that Van Dyke went public with his own alcoholism... and his recovery.[16]

"And Congressman Wilbur Mills." I added.

"Exactly. Do you relate to him, too?"

"I do."

Mills, the powerful head of the House Ways and Means Committee, had been making headlines for weeks, headlines like being apprehended by the U.S. Park Service police after jumping into Washington's Tidal Basin late one night with one

"Fanne Foxe," the stage name of an Argentinean stripper.[17] I liked the Congressman right away.

But what stopped me cold was the rest of the story: Mills had found recovery from alcoholism. I was impressed and encouraged by Mills' story. The fact that he and Van Dyke had found recovery, despite the societal biases of the 70s, lifted my heart like a happy kite in an easy breeze.

"BJ, you know, I think I have a shot at this, if it's a health issue, a medical problem, I can deal with that. I don't have a chance if it's only a moral issue."

I became part of the Division's program.

BJ put me in a therapy group that attracted five to eight people a week. A few couldn't seem to make a commitment to the group, but most stuck with it. Each of us had a common bond. And that bond, that demon made moot the differences among us, an important new lesson for me. Some were black, some white, some wealthy, a few practically on the street. But we were brothers. Several were even in AA, they told me. I met with BJ one-on-one once a week and went to my group every Wednesday night. I was on my way, but it was just a day at a time.

Those were big steps for me, yet still the summer just dragged on: hot, humid, devoid of worldly solutions or resolution. I did get another job– selling cars. Not Ferraris but Datsuns (now Nissan), and I sold some, too; but the job did not last long because I somehow talked my way back into a PR job again, an ill-fated move for it represented a return to my old ways, to the places in my life that had enabled my alcohol problem in the first place, my days of wine and roses.

No wonder, then, that I did not stop drinking. I went back and forth. I'd drink for a couple of weeks and then stop for a couple.

Shaving one morning, I noticed how florid my face had become. Now keeping score of my drinking, I noticed my tolerance for alcohol was dropping. I knew these were danger signals. I had soundlessly slid to the deadly bottom of Dr. Jellinek's chart. Still, I kept "coming back," as my new-found friends in the "recovery movement"– a rapidly expanding group of some of the most amazingly real folks I'd ever met– called it.

I kept coming back.

My last days of active alcoholism were during the Christmas season of 1973. I celebrated nothing. I had nothing, no family, no kids, no presents. My soon-to-be ex-wife had taken up with another man, I learned, and he had taken the toys I had bought for my kids that year and destroyed some of them. The pure meanness of that and the ostracism I felt forced me to isolate. That was the only thing I could think of to do to avoid violence. My feelings during those days were the worst I have ever experienced, before or since. The resulting nihilism was my own doing, of course. They were there but I was avoiding them and other people, friends– such as I had left– and my parents, sister, aunts, uncles and cousins, all folks who had meant so much to me in days long past.

I have no other understanding of that time other than that it was a form of retreat like a turtle pulling itself into its carapace. I isolated, still in the bottom, yet feeling like I was trying to tip-toe through a swamp, high-stepping over the quicksand.

Behaviors and attitudes of isolation and sinking anti-social feelings characterized my brand of alcoholism. There in the bottom, I had gotten so I could not read a newspaper beyond the headline and first paragraph. My mind was like a Mexican jumping bean on a hot summer sidewalk. When I wrote my name, I was never sure the signature would not expose my secret, the one evident in the slight palsied shake of my hand as I tried to write. Imagine a signature that looked like a drunk walking, and you've got the picture.

So I became a drone of denial, going through the motions of some instinct I must have inherited from my knuckle-dragging progenitors who doubtless hunted the wooly mammoth– just going from one hunt to the next– one drink to the next with no thought of why or what might follow. This informed my bottom– one with just two possible outcomes– recovery or a walking death.

Time crept. I had moved out. The marriage was done. I clung to a job, still going back and forth with drinking, Brick's "click" long-forgotten. Back and forth. Caught in the roulette wheel of The Bottom. The seasons changed, but I hardly noticed. Soon I was in a dark winter's cold, a soul cold. I endured that awful Christmas of 1973.

By the new year, no longer was there any Australia. No family either. We'd officially split. I moved to a small dumpy apartment in midtown. Suddenly and disturbingly, the path had become an ordeal, and I was way off center. A sense of foreboding loomed. The weight of years, and my ego-mania, were becoming too much. Suicidal ideation once more snaked around the serrated edges of my thinking.

The place I had moved to had been the parlor of an old Richmond Fan District home. The once-grand townhome had been turned into now-threadbare apartments. The place was full of strange characters. I avoided them. In a part of town known for its Bohemians, hipsters, free-spirited flower-children, dropouts, druggies and drunks, the old home was a high-toned flop house. And that's where The Bottom finally met me, where things all came to a head for me on a grim February day in 1974.

When I got up that Sunday morning, my thoughts came to me as through the ill-omened gloom around a crypt in the dark. I did what I always did on a weekend morning– I cracked open a cold beer. After a good pull, I put it down. I never picked it back up to drink. Instead I took it into the bathroom and poured it out. Quite bizarre, I told myself. I have never understood that. It was way off the old path. I didn't drink it. But it was not a physical thing– not like some friends I later met who had their throats seize up on them so they could no longer swallow. I just did not drink it. While pouring it out, I glanced at myself in the mirror and was shocked by the frightful thing I saw there.

I saw myself, of course, and I did not look so hot either. I looked tired, baggy-eyed, aging prematurely. But hovering behind me, I discerned in the mirror a dark presence. It silhouetted me. I felt a demented, psychotic melancholy about this presence, and the threat that came with it. Then I felt fear, an icy, deep-seated fear of the kind that will encase you like a prehistoric fly in amethyst, fear you just cannot flee after a certain point. I was at that point. I would later come to believe that this was some sort of supernatural manifestation, a warning from another place, one with no time. A baleful feeling crept over me. I turned away from the mirror to confront the presence. It was not there.

Afraid to look again into the mirror, I left that place and went to the next room. There for the first time in a long while, I knelt in prayer, and I asked God to show me the way out, the path to sobriety. Then I understood that those people I had met in recovery knew what they were talking about, and my choice was clear— their way, or that of the thing in the mirror.

The prayer took place at about 10:30 a.m., February 2, 1974. As of this writing I have not had a drink of alcohol in all the time since.

PART FOUR

Aftershocks

CHAPTER FOURTEEN

EARLY FEBRUARY'S GRAY COLD PERFECTLY FIT my mood. My confrontation with the 800-pound gorilla that had stood immutable for so long, waiting for his time, the evil I met that day in the mirror, along with the prayer that followed, soon led me on a great roller-coaster ride of blessings and curses. The ride was a mad mixture of wrong turns up one-way streets, successes offset by searing disappointments, loves gained, loves lost. None of that, however, came close to equaling the sheer joy I would now feel as I reclaimed my life– the life God had meant for me all along. There was a moral side to this adventure after all.

I started writing down everything that had just happened to me– the beginning of a journaling adventure that continues to this day.

Then, at another level, I experienced something beyond emotion or wishful thinking. I knew somehow the prayer had worked. I knew God had heard me.

God and I had a deal. It lived in that soul-level beyond human intellect and emotion. I got up from my knees knowing that recovery would take a lot of hard work, and I would need help. I would have to admit my error, wrongs and self-centeredness. False pride must yield to true humility, the kind that calls for the help of others, but whom I knew not.

I sat there for a while– What, not Why, driving my thinking– seeds of real self-examination. For the preceding six months I had been playing with sobriety. Being in BJ's program was the first step. It helped a lot, but I continued to bounce between self-deception and self-destruction. It took the Mirror to slam me into full reality. I would now either recover or die.

I would die, either directly or indirectly by becoming incapacitated, jailed or institutionalized with a "wet brain." There I would sit, a drooling, incoherent, forgotten, living dead man. Or I would live, as the prayer moved my thinking to a new place, one I never could have imagined.

The first tangible result of my prayer was not to sit there and take reality's punch, but to roust myself from mercurial irresolution and get to work on the What. This was new, my emotions now one hundred and eighty degrees from where they had been. Those feelings of newness and assertiveness were proof. They were answers to the prayer.

I eased into action, drifting through that dull Sunday as if floating on a light cloud. Somehow, I did not drink or even want to, a miracle in itself. But it was a still a grim day. I drove around a bit, then stopped at a drugstore with a grill and ate a bowl of soup. That's all I ate the whole day and night. I didn't like to eat anymore. I didn't talk to anybody. I didn't see or seek out anyone I knew. I was alone with a whole city around me.

The next morning I went to work. I always went to work, no matter how hung over I was. This time I was not. My now-clear blue eyes in the mirror I no longer feared, looked back at me. They reminded me of the resolution I had seen in BJ's weeks earlier.

I drove to my office through downtown traffic, accepting the fact that some other drivers were in just as big a hurry as I. This in itself was new behavior. Before— in the Why Me time— I would arrive at the office coiled like a diamond-back with ire at my fellow humans, all those lousy other drivers. But not this time.

Once settled, instead of working, I called the counselor I had been seeing in The Mosque. By then my friend BJ had left for greener pastures of work in the recovery business. Dennis was my new counselor. He was an ordained minister who had seen enough. He turned to the hard academic work of another advanced degree and passed the state's certification exam to become a substance-abuse counselor. When

I first got to know him, he worked with people like me while pursuing a doctorate in behavioral health. To this day, Dennis is one of the most good-hearted individuals I've known— dedicated to helping people who seek the path that does not stray.

That morning, Dennis was out of the office. I panicked, and when a woman counselor I didn't know very well came on the line, shock joined panic when I learned she knew a lot more about me than I had thought possible.

"I need to talk," said I.

"I know you do." She replied. "how soon can you get here?"

"Minutes," I said and rolled.

The office was just a few blocks away, still tucked into the side of The Mosque. I may have been asking the right questions finally, but I still skulked around that corner, making sure no one I knew was about to tag me going into The Division of Alcoholism Services.

Once there, I was met by the woman. With no dalliance for small talk, the Southern lubricant, the deceiver of feelings, she said:

"We haven't seen you around in a while, and you look like crap, so I know you've been drinking, right?"

"Umm, yeah, until yesterday anyway."

I told her what happened, struggling to keep eye-contact. "But I don't know what to do now," I said.

"I do. You're going to treatment," she said. "Wait here."

"I made a call," she said when she came back, "and you can go to the Alcoholism Treatment Unit at Riverside Hospital in Newport News."

"Yeah, I can do that," I said, my stomach starting to tighten as images of shock-treatment once more welled up within me. "Maybe we could set it up for the next week or so."

"No. Today," she said, no slack in her tone. "Right now. You're in need of medical attention."

Rattled, I agreed and left. I was afraid but focused. I resolved to go, no matter what. I still harbored notions of this situation I was in being but "a phase," something I would outgrow, like a teenager's pimples. I figured that, if I could dry out, get the lingo down and grasp the concepts of recovery, I could resume "normal" life, a lie that many rationalize much to their detriment. I would only discover "normal" much later.

Something new was working within me, and I was denying it. To find it, I needed to get to Newport News.

First I went back to my office and looked for my boss. He was not available. So I found his boss, interrupted what he was doing and said, "I have a problem with alcohol, Jack, and I've decided to do something about it."

His first response made me think he'd lost his voice or something. He didn't say anything, just sat there, a snarky smirk slowly crossing his Monday morning game face. I knew he did not like me particularly. The feeling was mutual. He was a career bureaucrat, stuck somewhere in his thinking in a trap with no true or false in it. So I pressed on, just for meanness, knowing that unvarnished facts would shock his bureaucratic equivocacy.

"I've been advised to go to a hospital unit that specializes in alcoholism treatment in Newport News, and I'm going right now. I'll be gone for three weeks."

"Very well," he said, and the smirk became the look of someone who'd just won the lottery. That was the moment I knew I no longer had a future in that organization, but we would go through the motions. So I got out of there.

"Screw 'em," I thought. I went to get my toothbrush and whatever.

Ready or not whether I knew it or not, recovery, the blessing of redemption— and a new life— had started. It would be later that I learned this; but I see it now: new unexpected behavior was to be a continuing and growing habit. As I practiced that habit, it grew along with my courage. I needed that, too. God's side of our deal? I think so.

I felt curiously elated, free, adventuresome but at the same time worried about the consequences of my actions. But that was old thinking. I quickly learned that whatever the consequences, they were better than the alternatives.

Then came yet another life-changing epiphany. Feelings like "worry" and fixations on "consequences" were becoming increasingly meaningless. I was being guided by a benevolent God, a concept, following a lifetime in church and even academic study of the Bible, that had never crossed my mind.

As for my previous failures, they no longer mattered. My Mad Hatter had never been to that hospital in Newport News. There I soon learned the basic principles of recovery. They presented the famous Twelve Steps of Alcoholics Anonymous to us. I learned that complexity was my enemy.

Of my earlier failures, my great friend the late Willie Steinbach was latter to say to me, "You let the simplicity of the program insult your intelligence."

He meant that my inclination to look for complexity in life, examining all the pluses and minuses, pros and cons, and then come to a supposedly rational conclusion, was getting in my way. Analysis paralysis resulted. Thus frustrated, I would turn to drink. But that was in a time now past. Had I reached a rational conclusion? I had never considered that some things cannot ever fully be understood.

"The most beautiful emotion we can experience," Albert Einstein wrote, "is the mysterious... he to whom this emotion is a stranger, who can no longer wonder and stand rapt in awe, is as good as dead, a snuffed-out candle."[18]

There I stood, at the crossroads of the mysterious. I could choose life or I could choose to be a snuffed-out candle. It was that simple, and that day I was changed, touched by the unknowable, letting go of the false notion that all was knowable. I chose life, and my little candle still burned, just a bit brighter, my path a little lighter. It shone its light on each footfall of the path.

CHAPTER FIFTEEN

BY 10:30 THAT MORNING, I HAD MY TOOTHBRUSH and stuff and was ready to go to Newport News, though little prepared for what lay in store for me. The thought crossed my mind to buy a six-pack of beer for the trip. Yeah, really. Nuts, huh? One more for the road, so to speak. But then I had heard somewhere that treatment centers such as the one I was headed to had detoxification programs featuring painful shots in the butt of vitamin B12 and other salubrious drugs if alcohol still lingered in one's system. So instead of the six-pack I popped a five-milligram tablet of Valium and rolled.

I had been introduced to Valium several years before by my psychiatrist friend, the one who hung up on me later. He told me it would help me during my period of not drinking and with depression. Not so. For me Valium was a rather unsatisfactory substitute: alcohol in solid form. In the rare circumstance when it was impossible to drink, I'd pop a Valium.

But now I was on a new road, and I felt a curious relief, convinced I was doing the right thing. Newport News is some seventy-five miles from Richmond, a straight shot eastward on Interstate 64 to J. Clyde Morris Boulevard and then another couple of miles to the hospital. Overhead, sleek fighter jets roared skyward from the nearby Langley Air Force Base. The closer I got to my destination, the more nervous I felt. Did they still do shock-treatments? Not likely, I told myself. Reality treatments were more like what I faced. I was right.

The day was not gray but clear– nearly perfect weather for early February– and sunny with no chill in the air, only the one still in my soul. I knew I was leaving something behind, a part of me that would never be re-visited. Leaving my old life, felt like the last time I had visited my spot under the sweet gum trees, Spanish moss swaying in the breeze.

The weather was talking to me. Nature's clear, crisp Virginia day was a portent. Little did I realize that what I was losing would soon be replaced by a new way.

Arriving at the large general hospital, I found a parking spot. The place was buzzing with activity as I made my way to the admitting office and announced my presence. "Admissions" was generic, typical hospital– lots of people sitting around, some slumped, napping, little kids fussing. Just another day at the office. Opposite them were about eight or ten admissions nooks, two of which were actually staffed. They were backed up by file cabinets, copiers, the miscellany of any office. I signed all the necessary papers, my signature still shaky as ever. An orderly appeared with a wheelchair.

"Thanks, but I can walk," I said, my naïveté about modern-day hospitals showing.

"Sorry, sir, but you have to ride," he said. "Hospital rules."

So, for the first time in my life, I sat in an actual wheelchair. It felt like a defeat. I was only thirty-three, and these things were just for old coots, right? I felt diminished and demeaned. At exactly that moment, in that lobby, my "treatment" began.

We rolled. First to a bank of elevators that led to what appeared to be like any other hospital– elevators in the middle with units extending out from there. The one I was headed to sported an enormous sign above the door that said "Alcoholism Treatment Unit." Well, so much for anonymity, thought I, as I rolled into my new home for the next three weeks. But by then, I was adapting. The wheelchair ride was actually cool. My chauffer, with whom I chattered along the way, was a real pro. He swerved at the last second to avoid other wheelchairs, or gurneys, some with gray people on them. I hoped they were not from the place where we were headed.

With a bit of flair we entered the Alcoholism Treatment Unit. A tall, raven-haired nurse quickly took charge of me. She told me she was a psychiatric nurse, took my vitals, and asked me endless questions, which she did in an understanding and very friendly way. Then she introduced me to a woman named Betty. Betty was a spry and lively middle-ager. Her eyes held a twinkle. I welcomed the sense of humor that augured.

Betty told me that she was going to be one of my counselors. She also told me that she was in recovery from alcoholism herself. Her length of sobriety was inconceivable to me– more than ten years, she said. I would learn that she was a legend in that part of Virginia among literally hundreds of people she had helped. Her expertise was really something to behold, and I was later to miss her enormously.

Next, I spoke with a youngish, friendly physician, a psychiatrist, who told me what I thought I had avoided by not drinking since Sunday morning. It was now mid-day Monday, and he said that the blood tests Nurse Raven-Hair had taken showed that I still had some alcohol in my system. I would have to be "detoxed" for a couple of days until he could be sure that the alcohol was gone. So I got the painful B-12 shots in the butt, after all. Having been one, I probably deserved a good pain in the ass.

Meanwhile, I began to mingle with the patients in a roomy, inviting common lounge area. The first guy I met had a connection in common. We were both from Richmond, had both worked for the same company, and of course both had the same drinking problems. Charlie was to become a good friend for many years. That day however he helped me to become comfortable with the– to use the professional's term– *milieu*.

We got some coffee and sat and talked in the common area. It was really where a nurses' station would have been. Only that unit did not seem to have one. The nurses wore civilian clothes and mingled with the patients. The *milieu* was a nicely appointed giant living room with a TV set at one end, and a collection of small tables and chairs at the other. Patient rooms were down two hallways at opposite ends of the area– one hall for women, the other for men. And the mix was balanced.

This facility, I learned, was a bit ahead of the curve of drug and alcohol treatment. It was a "Minnesota model" facility, one based on emphasizing the twelve-step program of drug-free abstinence pioneered by AA. Riverside Hospital was the first in the Hampton Roads and Richmond regions to adapt the model. That explained why about a third of the patients with me there were from Richmond. There was not a facility in Richmond at that point offering the same treatment philosophy. That would soon change, but I don't know what they did in Richmond before. Doubtless shock treatments, I mused. The trip, wheelchair, B-12 shot in the butt, and all, were worth it.

The next three weeks were carefully planned and structured. We rose early, made up our beds, showered, shaved, and dressed. We had breakfast, but first we did a brief and easy physical workout– nothing like the PT and five-mile runs I had experienced in the Army. Piece of cake.

The days were filled with combinations of physical recreation, lectures, and small groups in which we discussed each other's problems under the supervision of a counselor. We even had a young woman with rubber joints push us through a yoga class every other day. There I made a great discovery. My blood pressure, which had been high when I came in the door (I smoked, by the way), was actually lowered after fifty minutes of Hatha yoga stretching exercises. I was hooked.

That would turn out to be my introduction to the concept of a "positive addiction." The blood pressure drop along with the calm, relaxed feeling of well-being of a Yoga workout made me want to do more. So in my mind it was mildly addictive. I embraced it and looked for other positive activities that would contribute to improved health. I learned that I have an addictive personality. The logic, then, was inescapable: get into some positive addictions. Their benefits became characteristics of my incipient recovery.[19]

Yoga was but one of the activities of the program. Small group meetings were the centerpiece, the glue that held it all together. In one of the small-group experiences, we had to read an "inventory" of our lives that we had written out beforehand. Homework in a hospital. These inventories were supposed to link to our drinking or drugging experiences. Most did, except for one fellow– who would become my roommate about midway through the program. He was an affable chap. Ordinary looking. Average height of about 5'9– nothing to indicate he was probably a spy.

I surmised he had been a spy– or even a spymaster– by listening carefully to his inventory, his story. There was a fifteen-year gap in it. Along Interstate 64 just west of Newport News, lies an immense "Government Property" marked only by high fences topped by razor wire and loud signs saying Keep Out. Just beyond the razor-wired fences, lay a cleared area about twenty yards across. The cleared area was for vehicular traffic and for surveillance, I have always guessed, because the intimidating barrier encompassed Camp Peary– "The Farm," as the CIA calls its training facility.

My roommate, who said he was a "federal employee," told me he had joined the government at Camp Peary. But then his story continued as if without a gap 15 years later. Our group "facilitator," and some of us, too, confronted him on it but got nowhere. No wonder he was in an alcoholism treatment center. Lots of secrets with nowhere to go.

At Riverside, we were introduced to AA. The unit required our participation. People in AA from the Newport News community came in and conducted regular AA meetings with us. Some were closed to just our group and those volunteers who came in. Others were open community AA meetings. Either way, the meetings were long-established examples of people helping each other through the power of the shared experience, fellowship and learning to follow the famous 12 steps of AA.

Those steps were always read at the beginning of each meeting. The gatherings usually numbered 35 or so attendees, people of all ages from all walks of life with no discrimination, no "profiling" or any of the other cultural pretenses of the society that surrounded us and which many of us blamed for facilitating the fixes we had gotten ourselves into in the first place.

Some meetings feature one or two speakers who will share their "experience, strengths and hope" with the larger group. Others will be general discussion groups. A chairperson presides over either speaker or discussion meetings, and a general format is followed with minor variations among groups.

Paralleling those meetings, group therapy, and individual counseling, my care included meetings with my psychiatrist, one of two medical directors of the unit. Those meetings were pretty comprehensive. The doctor surprised me with his ability to nail troubling aspects of my behavior. For example, slowly over the years, so slowly I had not noticed, I had developed a tendency to avoid direct confrontation with anything other than the pleasant patterns that fed my addiction. That's why— when asking me about my children and what I was going to do when I got home about seeing them and redeveloping relationships with them— he got no answer.

I had no clue, but more than that, I subliminally covered the whole issue with denial and rather elegantly constructed procrastination. The doctor forced the issue and made me deal with it by direct phone calls, and a promise to continue the process when I got home. I agreed. I did. It was uncomfortable. But it was effective and would lead to considerable drama a few months later.

Nursing care focused on the physical. I caught a cold. Took Tylenol. Drank orange juice. Got over it— all things I would not have done before… except drink it away. Alcohol had remarkable germ-killing properties, I had reasoned.

In a deeper sense, the nursing staff was highly professional and knew their patients and what might happen during our stay. We had a guy walk out, for example. The charge nurse called the police who apprehended him across the way in a beer joint in a shopping center getting drunk.

One evening after supper we all gathered to watch a movie, *The Days of Wine and*

Roses, the Jack Lemmon movie that I had liked so much in earlier years. The reason I liked it is that I identified with the suave and urbane character Lemon played, a PR guy like me. I had wanted to be like Jack. What I had forgotten by that evening, of course, were the parts of the movie I had denied because of its tragic second half.

In the film Lemmon plays Joe Clay. He marries Kirsten, played by Lee Remick. Kirsten is a teetotaler, Joe a regular drinker. He introduces her to the joys of alcohol. Things go well for them. Joe keeps getting promotions. Kirsten has a beautiful baby girl. The American dream begins.

But– "They are not long, the days of wine and roses;"[20] and Joe's and Kirsten's drinking inevitably progresses into active alcoholism. Joe loses the best job he's ever had. Kirsten becomes an embittered, hopeless drunk, their daughter, Debby, a vulnerable, helpless victim.

After trying hard and failing often, Joe finally finds sobriety in AA. Kirsten leaves, unable to stop, herself. And in the end, after Joe has stabilized, gotten an OK job and is providing a home for Debby, late one night Kirsten comes home and asks Joe to accept her back. But she says she wants to return to the old days, the good times, the days of wine and roses.

Things were better then, she asserts, because she's an addict. She is blinded to truth by her drinking. Joe says he cannot go back to those days and will not reconcile unless Kirsten finds recovery. She turns and walks out. In the final scene, Joe watches through a window as she leaves, walking up the street towards a place that's still open that late. Its garish red sign says "Bar."

I had seen the film three times following its debut in 1962. But the film I saw that night in Riverside Hospital's Alcoholism Treatment Unit was not the same one I had seen all those years earlier. I had scourged the ending from my memory. I did not want to entertain its sadness. I learned that night how powerful denial can be– so powerful that it can kill.

Another reality hit me hard that evening. After the movie, we were all just hanging out, drinking coffee, chatting, winding down from the day. But with no warning anything was wrong, one of our number walked across the way to the coffee area, and fell to the floor. He looked gray and shook. I thought he was dying. Then I recognized what seemed to be a seizure of some kind. I knew that because I had gone to high school with a fellow who was epileptic and went into a seizure right in front of me in the hallway between classes one day. But this was different.

The charge nurse and one other nurse were there instantly. Using a flat wooden spatula, one of them made sure that her patient would not swallow his tongue. It was frightening to behold, but the nurses quickly turned it into a teaching experience. What had just happened to him could have happened to any of us, and the episode was a potential killer, the nurses said. Sure, I had read that alcoholism could kill, but I glossed over that thought, believing alcoholism would kill "hopeless" street cases, like one in particular I would soon come to know. But I didn't think that could happen to me. Not me. Yet there it was, death's shade, death's fore-shadow, death's possibility made real for me within minutes. Coincidence? I think not. Some meaningful messages come in strange packages at odd times.

The guy came around pretty quickly. A nurse took him aside to continue care and make sure he was stable. In the meantime, the other nurses kept talking to the rest of us in small clusters about what could happen to active alcoholics. It frightened me. I did not want to have that happen to me... or anyone around me. Yet it would.

CHAPTER SIXTEEN

GRIM FEBRUARY MORPHED INTO BRIGHT, BREEZY March, and I felt just as new as the weather. Somehow, I'd hit the reset button, and the closer I got to my time to leave Newport News, the more my feelings came to the surface, no longer stupefied by alcohol, hidden under quilts of guilt, or innervated by nutty rationalizations. But minus my alcoholic buffer, I was afraid.

Fear had crept in once I resolved to "make some changes." I had troubles back home, troubles that would not be fixed while disembodied by 75 miles of telephone lines, but which soon would be in my face. They would become my next step into recovery.

As far as I knew, my house was occupied by my wife, her boyfriend and my kids. It was also in foreclosure. I knew I could return to my job but I was sure it would be short-lived, recovery or no. And the bank was after my car for late payments. I did not know where any of this stood. I braced myself for the worst when I returned home.

Meanwhile, I continued to deal with those issues as best I could by telephone as my doctor, the nurses, and my fellow patients had urged. Immediate and direct confrontation of such problems was a unique concept to me at that time, but it was overdue and necessary for long-term recovery. One of the eye-openers of AA that I learned from the people who volunteered their time to share with us, was in AA Founder Bill Wilson's book, *As Bill Sees It*:

"It has often been said of AA that we are interested only in alcoholism. That is not true. We

have to get over drinking in order to stay alive. But anyone who knows the alcoholic personality by firsthand contact knows that no true alky ever stops drinking permanently without undergoing a profound personality change." [21]

There are people who will say that it is impossible for an individual to experience a total change of personality or character. My experience belies that, as do the experiences of many others whom I've had the privilege to see find new lives of recovery.

For me it began with the treatment center and all of its salubrious adventures, the small groups, exercise, and recreational therapy and, of course, yoga. I resolved to stop smoking but did not immediately. I did, however, begin to get myself back in shape, having seen once sober how out of shape I was. I disliked that because I'd always been active. I played tennis, I jogged, mowed grass, body-surfed with my kids in the surf and managed to stay in pretty good shape.

But alcoholism's slow slog, its death-march coda, took me far from those places. You could see it in my face. I had come to look like a tomato. When I renewed my driver's license some months later, they gave me my new license. But they gave me my old one too. I saw two different people. The new me looked pretty good, smiled at the camera, looked directly into the lens with no evasion or dissembling. But the old me was puffy-faced with an off-putting expression. One side of my face was not shaven as well as the other and there was a strange sheen to my skin. My tie was slightly askew. I still keep the old license as a reminder: the mug shot of a person who no longer exists.

Other indicators of "profound personality change" came about in the multi-disciplinary process of the program. In my group sessions, my assumptions about life– the ones I had thought so effective– were dismantled a piece at a time by my fellow group members. I learned to be teachable again at age thirty-three. Thus commenced my recovery– recovery of health, thought, spirit, and emotion. Yet a strange brew of fear and courage accompanied me as I went home. The time came, faster than I wanted it to.

Like molasses in the cold, my fears oozed but soon loosened with spring's advent. As temperatures warmed, circumstances lost their edge. Their daunting, taunting myrmidons began to see the chariots of fire now covering my back. My spirit was awakening from years of depression. Nature's insights inspired.

As I drove through a suburban office park late one afternoon, the winds picked up as the skies darkened heralding an early-spring storm. Surrounded by the trappings of commerce, I saw something I had never noticed before. Petals from a large copse of Bradford Pear trees in front of a nearby office complex looked like snow as they blew across the roadway before me. A storm was coming, and for once it was not a mental storm, but a marvelous show of nature. The modest tempest's strong leading gusts seemed to blow away the detritus of my stingy old thinking. I felt stronger. Fear was still there. But strength bolstered my ability to accept and deal with it.

Fear is like happiness. It comes and goes. I don't. I remain in my own skin. Me. Home, though, was now a dead space. I faced an empty house, no longer a home. Everything not attached was gone. The kitchen phone appeared to have been pounded through the drywall into the empty space behind it, still attached to a now dead phone line. There was no electricity. The only things alive were two little cats that had been left behind. They were frightened and starving. They'd apparently been abandoned when everything had been removed, left to subsist on bugs in a house now of just ghosts. The house had been left in that state by my soon-to-be-ex and her putative boyfriend. I have no idea when, nor had I any idea where, she was, or my children.

So startling was the scene before me, and the situation it evinced, that I knew I faced an uphill battle to find a semblance of balance in life again. While my two friends who accompanied me waited, I went around back, sat on the stoop's steps and cried. All of my stuff— clothes, books, prized and close meaningful photos and memorials to a past that now seemed as far away as the Hale-Bopp Comet— was gone.

With me that day was Tommy, one of my best friends, and my mother-in-law, who would soon prove to be an ally too, because she had been left equally in the dark as to what was going on. This serendipity was one of those blessings only a benevolent God could have bestowed. At the very least it told me I was on the right path and had not been one-hundred percent wrong in the relationship, which I had allowed myself to believe I was.

The house was a well-kept brick rancher on a sedate suburban street that dead-ended on the edge of a pleasant little woodland. It was in a subdivision called "Stuart's Ridge," eponymous with the Confederate cavalry leader who had traversed the area in his famous circumlocution of McClellan's seemingly inept Federal army, the one that could have shortened the Civil War by three years had he not been intimidated by Lee's and Stuart's aggressive rebels.

So for me, the history buff, I loved it. In many ways it seemed the perfect neighborhood. The old busy-body diagonally across the street, the one who was always popping up one of the slats in her ever-tightly-closed blinds to see what was going on, was still at her post, I noticed.

At the house, just before I contemplated murder, I noticed the subpoenas. They papered the front door. They announced foreclosure, suits filed for late payments and who-knows-what-else. But I was in no mood for rational thinking or behavior that day. Meanwhile Ms. Slats was getting a real workout because I kept turning around to give her the evil eye, the only fun I was to have all day.

Next, there was the mail. Piles of it, most of which was either useless junk or bad news, like what I had ripped off the door.

These concentrated confrontations with the so-called real world got the best of me. Looking at reality through lenses unfiltered by a mood-altering chemical was all new to me. Thus it followed that, even though accompanied by two good friends, I began to feel a monumental plume of rebellious anger arise in my being unlike any I had ever felt before. That's why I understood and contemplated murder– much better than suicide, about which I was ambivalent. But I didn't give a damn. I really didn't, even though in the 19th Century calculus I'd inherited, the family name was soon to be ruined in perpetuity on the courthouse steps one fine summer day, or at least so I fancied. The monster bulged against the closet door and murder made sudden sense. It was then that I remembered the moral expiation from *The Godfather*: When Michael Corleone coolly shot to death an enemy of the Family, a New York City police captain, it was "just business, nothing personal," he said. Worked for me.

So there I was, massaging a murderous impulse, when I arrived at the only way I could find at the moment to deal with the reality before me. I took the legal papers from the door, grabbed up all the mail, and carried it all into the back yard and set it on fire. Had not the ancients appeased their demons in the same way? I was truly their son that day.

Then I left, never to return to that place. But still the Luger waited.

CHAPTER SEVENTEEN

AFTER I MADE SURE THE LITTLE KITTENS were fed and in a safe new home, I turned my back on what had been my own home, and my anger of that awful first day back from Newport News subsided. I was in my beloved hometown again, surprised when I realized I now had an opportunity to start a new life. What I had learned in the hospital made me new, and wreaking mayhem was replaced by something closer to rational thinking. Life likewise seemed a surprise, at least for the moment.

I began to see, feel, and touch the world again: grass, birds, rain, sun, even moonlight, stars, and bugs– all things my quixotic egomaniacal quest of self-destruction had obscured. They became real again. It was like seeing them for the first time.

Ironic that now I used no chemical to sully life's truth, for before I had personalized the DuPont Company's old ad catchphrase, "Better Living through Chemistry." My icons of those days– the worldly pursuits, the grabbing at straws, the telling of tall tales– hung like old fox-hunting prints, no more romance in them, on lifeless dull walls becoming dimmer with each passing day. While all had looked gray just a month before, now light glimmered in my life. Soon, however, a new and darker cloud would cast its ominous shadow. My children were being kept from me, hidden, I knew by whom but not where. Nor did even my mother-in-law knew.

My wife and I had a checkered relationship over nearly ten years. We had started off well, but just as slowly as my alcoholic progression, the edges began to fray.

When I first looked back, I thought it was all me— I was causing the marriage's deterioration.— but I was telling myself a lie.

In my work in Newport News, it was all me, though. I wrote a personal inventory, highlighted by stunts like my lost rental car incident years earlier. Or my final Labor Day drinking fling, my last big holiday weekend before I crashed into the real world. Instead that was the day I crashed my own car and two rental cars while earning two reckless-driving tickets. Those events and others like them predominated in my "personal inventory."

Getting this junk out on the table, told to others who understood and were going through the same process, was an early step in recovery. These exercises underscored for me the truth that every story has two sides. But it would take a while before the drama of that other side would take center stage. Meanwhile I began to share my stories on other stages.

The closer I got to Christmas that year, the more I remembered, and I began to share these stories with my newfound friends in the recovery movement. The experience was like an extension of therapy. The surprise was that I discovered laughter again— laughter at myself especially. It is indeed the best medicine.

I remembered the time I had been picked to be a "Wise Man" in my church's Christmas pageant. It was on Christmas Eve. That year it fell on a Friday, which meant I got to leave my job downtown at noon. I drank my way home, stopping at two or three suppliers' office parties on the way. When it came time to suit up as a Wise Man I was pretty well lit. But the show must go on, and I soon found myself walking onstage accompanied by two friends, now the Three Kings from the strange Orient.

As I knew from my teen years, stage lights are hot. The hotter they got, the more stressed got I, while the audience of proud parents, kids, grandparents, and neighbors all beamed. Seems I had not had a chance to go to the restroom before entering stage left, and that was fast becoming a problem.

The experience became the longest Christmas Pageant ever. The fact that Middle Eastern kings wore robes of fine wool during the cold of December exacerbated my distress under the hot lights of suburban American stagecraft. This became drama within drama, proceeding at its stately pace, while I recalled someone once telling me one of the legends of devoted beer-drinkers everywhere: "If you don't go when you have to, your bladder could explode."

I had always prided myself on resourcefulness, however, and I plugged the pressing problem into my crisis-management planning mode: I could exit stage left for a few minutes. But, no, that just wasn't in the script, given the possibility of lightning strikes and whatnot. I could tough it out, but that was a fast-fleeting fancy. I couldn't make it. Alfred Hitchcock reportedly once said: "Always make the audience suffer as much as possible." Only this time it was the actor who was suffering.

I decided to do what I had to do. Since my long, and now even hotter, wool robe went all the way to the tops of my shoes, I would "go" a little bit, and it would run down my leg and into a shoe. Thus would I prevent an exploding bladder, and the audience would be spared the unscripted spectacle.

So, after dutifully delivering my myrrh, or whatever it was, I dropped back a little and implemented active crisis management. It worked, but I left a telltale puddle. I was a wreck by the end of the thing. I felt every eye in the house was on me and they knew. Of such power was my paranoia that I invented alibis right away– I would say: "Inadvertently I took a bottle of water with me in my rush to get onstage, and I'd left the top off." Or something like that.

But nothing happened. Once the curtain closed and the house lights came up, I did a sort-of swoopy ballet move while exiting, deftly and surreptitiously mopping up the oasis with my trailing robe. Then I fast-tracked out of there. Back home, I braced myself for what my wife would say. Nothing much, as it turned out, except: "Why was your face so red up there? Are you catching a cold?"

I had dodged another bullet, but I began to suspect I was running out of dodges. Such dances of denial were getting habitual, and I was good at them. But that would not last. This was becoming truly hard work, and pretty much defined the months leading up to my trip to Newport News. I blamed myself 110 percent for it all.

As I told the cathartic stories, however, the day came as it must when I learned that all was not my fault. I learned the whole truth when I recalled another, more frightening story.

While still a family— at least in name— we were trying to keep things together "for the kids." But for Ms. Slats we put on quite a show one of those last days before the crash— my bottom's bottom. We attracted a fire truck and two police cars followed by an ambulance— all with red and blue lights blazing, roaring down our quiet street like some kind of civic blitzkrieg— and all because I had called 911 thinking my then-wife was trying to take her life.

I had taken my young son to see his grandfather for a while. I had not had a drink in several days. The day had dawned hopeful. But when my little boy— he was one-and-a-half then— and I came home, my daughter was walking around wringing her hands, a jarring look of worry on her three-and-a-half-year-old face.

"What's wrong, honey," I asked.

"Mommy won't get up," she said, her direct young innocence radiating worry.

Her mom lay on the sofa in a tight fetal knot. Her color was normal, but she would not respond to me, her head buried in the sofa's cushion, hands tightly clenched.

Her hands— so tightly coiled their joints were white— set off alarms in my mind. It took considerable strength, but I was finally able to pry one hand open. She clutched what appeared to be small pills, some crushed to powder.

"Is Mommy going to be alright, Daddy," my little girl asked.

"We'll try to make sure she is. I'm going to call the rescue squad."

It seemed hours later that I paced the emergency room floor— in the same hospital where the children had been born— waiting. My mother-in-law, whom I had called, took the kids to her home, and I followed the ambulance soon after a police sergeant enlightened me on "domestics," as they call slat-raising performances like ours.

"We see this occasionally, Mr. Blue," he said, a serious look on his face, his right hand resting on his holstered weapon.

"The crushed pills were apparently just aspirin. It's an act. She was trying to send you a signal. Has there been trouble between you?" he asked. His demeanor had become avuncular but he still had an eye out for trouble.

"Yes," I replied, "I'm afraid our marriage is on the rocks, and neither one of us knows what exactly to do."

In the emergency room waiting area, the policeman's observation was verified when the white-coated young doctor came out of the treatment area. "It was just aspirin, but we pumped her stomach just in case," he said.

"She'll be all right to go home in a while," he said, "but I would recommend that she seek some counseling."

That never happened, and home life deteriorated like bubbles on the beach at ebb tide. Now here I was trying to get at least my part back together. The experience was the turning-point that showed me this was a shared, co-dependent kind of thing that was going on. Recollection of the episode became a milestone on my road to recovery, for it confirmed for me what I had heard the professionals say: "Alcoholism is a family disease."

PART FIVE

Lesser Simians

CHAPTER EIGHTEEN

WITH THE 800-POUND GORILLA DEFLATED, the Luger back in place, the Mad Hatter had taken a walk, and I gave no more thought to the grim image in the mirror.

These recollections unfolded for me as I ruminated on my recent past. They instructed my new walk on the formerly distant shore. My self-talk had turned from the webs of dysfunction I had woven following the day of the Mirror and the search for nine-millimeter death. It had taken years. But that's what it takes for some. The new shore had its shoals, but they held little fear. I came to call them the Lesser Simians.

Implicit in the prayer– the one I knelt for that day in 1974– was the message that I had much work to do, and I wasn't sure I understood what that meant. If it meant going to gatherings of folks in recovery, sharing stories, experiences and strengths, I was there. If it meant helping others, I was on it. Meanwhile old friendships fled, but newer, truer ones grew. Even all that was not the real hard work, though. The tough stuff would come soon enough, and it meant dealing with the wreckage of my past.

Sixteen years sliding down the Jellinek Curve– the bad side– had left broken relationships, worldly losses and near-tragic consequences of some pretty bad behavior. They reflected patterns of thinking. The changes in brain chemistry a doctor would later explain to me meant embedded self-destruction. Those changes portended the slow, baleful, drooling kind of death I saw some experience. Just because I had put the plug in the jug, the consequences continued. My Lesser Simians epitomized those consequences.

I lost the job I had walked out of to go to Newport News. No surprise there. I didn't like it anyway, but the loss was hard to handle.

I had to give my car back to the bank. They wanted their money. I didn't have any. Simple. So I gave them the car and found a cheap old heap to drive, a traditional badge of early recovery. It was an American Motors Ambassador, an all-white full-sized sedan with a 350-cubic-inch V-8 engine, black-wall tires and little hubcaps. In other words, it looked, and moved, like a police car.

And late one night, I rather aggressively wheeled in to an all-night convenience store for a cup of coffee and scared the hell out of a suspicious gaggle of homies hanging out there. They scattered like the wind when they saw me, because I wore a gray suit, white shirt and red-striped tie, an outfit that screamed The Law in mufti. It was little moments like that that leavened life's unending challenges some in those days.

Reality brought me back. I did not want to think about the house. It was sold at foreclosure, back then a rarity, and one that carried lots of Southern-style baggage with it: shame and stigma, the things of catty susurrations in the corner, just like I'd overheard as a kid.

The good physician I was about to get to know would encourage me to keep on going, regardless of the consequences, and gradually life would become easier to navigate. The sometimes scary Lesser Simians were actually "growth opportunities," as one of my more optimistic fellow recoverees called them. Working through these opportunities would lead to subtle, or perhaps not so subtle, changes in behavior and thinking. However, that did not mean I was suddenly a "happy, joyous and free" new me. I had drunk to maintain "happy," I thought. But real recovery means learning to take the bad and the good with equanimity.

I became like *"Chef Inspecteur Jacques Clouseau de la Sûreté,"* Peter Sellers playing the protagonist in the hilarious Pink Panther movie series. When his character, Clouseau, would return home after a tough day *à la Sûreté,* he entered his gentlemen's redoubt as if without a care in the world. And then, while in the midst of a routine act of homecoming, like flipping through the mail, or putting away groceries, his house man Cato would suddenly leap from nowhere like some unhinged deus ex machina and assault his boss.

The exercise, of course, was meant to keep le Chef Inspecteur on his toes, ready for any contingency. I had to be just as vigilant, watching myself, my thinking, my emotional state, for my life depended on it. Thus the difference between me and Clouseau was that his surprise set-to would end hilariously, while any sudden successful assault of the urge to drink again would end tragically for me. So, like Clouseau, I learned to stay on my toes. And with the passage of time, my irrational Cato moments diminished.

By the time Starbucks was just getting popular, it was too late. I had already found my place. It was a smoky pancake house that stayed open all night. It attracted all kinds. I once saw the Rev. Jerry Falwell and his son in there. At the other end of the spectrum were dudes driving tricked-up Caddies with faux-gold grills, bikers, families eating ice cream— just about every one of the area's demographics.

That included the recovery demographic. People in various stages of recovery gravitated there nightly. There were old timers and new comers. All gave support and comradery. Lifelong friendships were made, but I also had friends whose lives were not so long because they died of direct alcohol abuse, overdose or the wide variety of medical problems abuse could cause.

One summer night in 1975, I sat with my physician friend.

"Remember that alcohol is a depressant drug," he said." Indulged daily in larger-than-normal quantities, it changes brain patterns."

I learned that just ten to fifteen years of continuous drinking of alcohol— even without the "ism" appended— would result in profound changes in brain chemistry.

"These changes will produce subtle— or sometimes not so subtle— changes in behavior and thinking," he said, "and some of those changes could take a long time to reverse."

I took his knowledge to heart and began to look at myself anew. I had some unraveling work to do. His counsel showed me the way. But first I must get things out in the open. Talk about them, but being careful with whom.

I learned that these brain changes could include clinical hysteria– not the screaming-meemies, but something more like magical thinking– thinking that reflected the belief that the same behavior would magically produce different results when repeated. In her bestseller, *The Year of Magical Thinking*, Joan Didion calls it "delusionary thinking, the omnipotent variety..."[22]

"Sounds like the chick who marries the wrong guy thinking 'I'll change him,'" I said, "as if that would really happen, that would be 'magical.'"

"Exactly," my doctor friend replied.

"... thinking as small children think," Didion wrote, "as if my thoughts or wishes had the power to reverse the narrative, change the outcome."[23]

"Ironic, isn't it," I said. "That's exactly how I approached my marriage, and look what happened."

"You both did it," the doc said. "You both were going to change the other."

I had to agree. New clarity was a specialty of those gatherings at the coffee place.

My exchange with the doc demonstrates the value and power of the shared experience, a characteristic of recovery groups and the friendships they spawn, attributes that add up to what one really needs to do to recover and stay that way. You see, there are many times in the active alcoholic's life when the dark side will tell us a drink is the only thing that will help. The key is to stick with the process, though. Those folks I had known who had dropped out of sight? That's the group most of the deaths I would learn of came from. They had dropped out of the process and flown from recovery's hive.

I'd gotten to know a talented graphic artist whose reputation as one of the ad business' best preceded him. That, added to his whiz-bang high profile in AA, impressed me. I made it a point to get to know him, to learn how he was doing it, staying sober and happy with it.

So I watched him. He readily shared his experience, the drinking and how he stopped, with all who asked. He worked with newcomers on the new life without alcohol. He appeared to thrive. But one day, he just dropped off the 'scope. No more at the coffee house. No one had seen him. Others said he had lost his job. Some said no, it was his divorce that was bothering him. Whatever it was, he was gone.

About three months later, I ran into him. He was sitting at the lunch counter in a neighborhood drugstore eating a grilled cheese sandwich with a glass of water.

"How are you, Ding?" I said.

I saw his answer rather than heard it. As he mumbled something like "not so hot... under the weather... getting divorced," my eyes saw the real answer: his bloodshot eyes added to his unshaven face and the slump of a loser told me how he really was: hung-over.

"You're drinking again."

"Some... and, hey I gotta eat up and get back to work now."

"Where?"

"Little place down the street."

"Call me if you need to talk, Ding."

"Yeah. Thanks."

He was gone.

And that was the last I saw of him. A few weeks later I heard he had committed suicide.

I told my doctor friend about him. He already knew.

"Good example. You'll see more. They 'get it' but only superficially," he said. "That's why the long-term recovery rate is so low. Some just don't understand how profound and how dangerous chemical dependency of any kind can be... and how much deep work they must do to avoid what happened to Ding.

"You'll see it again. Take it as a lesson of this life."

Things like that got my attention. But they motivated me, and once I grasped what my friend was saying, these new ways of handling life, their ebbs, flows, and dangers, a new light glimmered in a mind dimmed by chemical twilight.

Clarity of thinking made life slowly get better, if not easier. The new ways reflected a time-honored adage I had first seen on a desk in an old office building– the desk of Alice, a friend of recovery to hundreds, if not thousands, of people who for now nearly fifty years has greeted newcomers to AA in Richmond. The saying was molded in brass, embraced by a polished solid dark wood frame, and sat front and center on her desk at "The Club," a redoubt of recovery and fellowship for all comers. It read:

"There is nothing that can happen to me today that God and I together cannot handle."

After my confrontation with the demon in the mirror, and following years of dodging simians great and lesser, what was and was to come were really no more than just dealing with life on life's terms.

One time I presumed God had told me to take a certain course, and I failed miserably. After losing my job, I tried all sorts of things to get reemployed but nothing seemed to work. The one that I thought would, and believed to be divinely inspired, had me moving to the resort city of Virginia Beach, where I would become a resort-property mogul.

As luck would have it– which I was sure was not really luck but the well-planned result of my usual well-oiled (but not juiced) resourcefulness– I soon met a fellow mogul. He was a real estate broker whose appropriately appointed office– old nautical stuff on the walls, bowls of sea shells and sand tracks across the hardwood floor– was just a block off of the confluence of Hampton Roads and the Chesapeake Bay. It was ripe for redevelopment– a sprawling waterside strip of older homes, duplexes and quadriplexes put up in earlier times and now crying out for newness and glitz, their shingled exteriors reflecting the results of the unrelenting erosion of sun, wind, Bay spray, northeasters, hurricanes, and flooding.

The mogul made me an offer to join him in redeveloping nothing less than large chunks of Virginia Beach and Norfolk, which bordered the Beach close by. He would lead; I would sell. So I went back to Richmond to get my mogul on, and it was later that week that God entered the picture. I caught a snippet of the Rev. Pat Robertson's 700 Club on TV just as he was intoning one of his signature prayers. With eyes tightly-closed and the intensity of a fervid Old Testament prophet, he proclaimed God's power to lift "you" out of a worldly mire and into a divine destiny. "You," was what I heard and took to heart. Never mind that millions world-wide were hearing the same "you," he was talking to me, and I promptly took it to mean grab the brass ring and join the mogul. So I did.

But by the time I got back to Norfolk and his "office," someone else was there. They said they had never heard of the guy, and I could tell they were lying. Something was wrong with the picture, and common sense paid me a rare visit. The mogul was apparently pulling some kind of con... or was as self-deluded as I.
I left, hopes dashed, yet understanding anew the chemical contortions my own mind could conjure. Grandiose thinking in early recovery went to the top of my list, the cognitive behavior watch-list.

A few days after the mogul debacle, I met with a wise lady-friend, a successful businesswoman from my church. We were having lunch at Byram's, then one of Richmond's landmark restaurants, a place where business deals were done, celebrations flourished and where I had made merry at many a milestone for more than thirty years.

The lobsters still sulked in their tank just inside the entry alcove, creatures "of little brain," as Christopher Robin once said of Pooh. I had trouble eating them because they seemed so forlorn; and only once did I, just before celebrating my doomed marriage. So there I was again, working on being a new man, with a friend who, not only helped me discover women as real friends, but also offered wise counsel.

"Did you hear yourself?" she said.

"What?"

"You said you 'decided that God wanted you to do this'?"

"I did, didn't I?"

"Yes. What I hear is that you made that up and maybe worse than that, you put words in your Creator's mouth."

So magical thinking can mess up a business plan, but it can also invite sudden lightning strikes. Message received. That epiphany though was mild compared with some of the other situations I would face during my first year of sobriety.

My brand of magical thinking magnified reality and framed it with beautiful, seductive auras– clouds back-lit in bright pastels that overtook reality and made it bigger than life. There was no muffler on my emotional pipes, no brakes on the near train-wreck that had become my exciting new life. But I had begun a program to change.

What I wanted in a real job was unrealistic. I jumped at the chance to be a "mogul," for example, because I needed a boost for my wounded ego. That was not to be. Instead what I really needed, I got. A beginner's job as a desk clerk in a hotel. It turned out to be one of the best things I've ever done.

And they actually paid me to do this "work" stuff? What a concept, one that had eluded me in my over-the-top, ego-driven, drug-induced megalomania.

I did start at the top in one sense, the best hotel in downtown Richmond at the time, the place to see and be seen by politicians, entertainers, business elites– Hotel John Marshall, a grand example of neo-classical dignity built in 1929 with more than 400 rooms and a ballroom that could seat 1,200, big for its time.

My experience there was worth well more than the regular paycheck,. First, I got promoted pretty fast, from desk clerk to assistant manager to senior assistant manager to convention sales manager. That was a fast-track. It happened over about 18 months and helped me realize that the loss of self-esteem of active alcoholism was reversible– if you stopped drinking, of course. It also proved another aphorism of recovery, and life: you get what you need not what you want.

Among the most important things I got from that job, and perhaps its most impactful experience, was the exposure to groups of people I never would have met, known or understood. Everyone from United States Senators, Presidential candidates, entertainment celebrities to housekeepers, maintenance men and bell hops. I learned that there is great worth in all people, and very probably more so on the lower rungs of that scale than otherwise.

At the beginning, however, the experience was off-putting. I felt the job was beneath my dignity, the same dignity with which I would whiz on a Nativity scene while hundreds of the faithful were watching. The what-ifs dogged me, too. What if some of my former cronies actually saw me there doing what a desk clerk does when I had been "somebody" in the corporate citadels back in The Day?

I willed myself to get over such self-puffery through sheer mental *force majeure*. And I did– fast. After about two weeks, I was walking in for the three-to-twelve shift. It was the first real summer day of the year, beautiful but hot. When I walked into the grand traditional lobby, buzzing as usual with a great variety of people, bellmen hustling, the important and the ordinary to-ing and fro-ing, I saw my boss at the desk sharing a laugh with a regular; and I knew I was exactly where I needed to be. It was fun, and the people were wonderful.

My boss, a short jovial black man with a world-class sense of humor, and I would mess with people's minds after I had "gotten" the routine there. Once we rigged a phony check-in form for one "Stein, Dr. Frank N.," address "Transylvania." We sent the part of the form to the telephone switchboard operators in case Herr Dr. Stein were to get a call. We included a non-existent room number. Then we used an outside phone line we had behind the desk to call the hotel and ask: "Yasss. May I pliz speaking mit Herr Doktor Stein?"

The switchboard's supervisor, a self-important, bossy busy-body with zip for a sense of humor, called us and informed us that we had put the wrong room number on Dr. Stein's check-in form. We told her that was not true. Dr. Stein's room was a newly renovated one and had a new number.

"Please put Dr. Stein's call through," my boss said, "and if you fail, page him." Click.

The die was cast and there was no turning back. Time ceased. Our jobs flashed before us as we waited. If she really did it, the big boss would know why... and probably who, too.

The paging system sounded though all public places in the hotel. A low-grade electrical hum presaged the message. My boss and I got out of sight of the general public. The speakers came to life with an authoritative timbre, and everyone heard it:

"Paging Dr. Stein, Dr. Frank N. Stein, please call the Operator."

Titters and knowing glances flashed about, but most folks pretended not to notice. We had pulled it off and broke into muffled guffaws, still in the back room sneaking peeks.

Later, the hotel's general manager cornered us and told us with a slight smirk and a glint in his eye "someone" had pulled this "stunt," and while he thought it was pretty creative, the supervisor did not get it, but everyone else did, so would we please inform whoever pulled this off not to use the public address system for their practical jokes?

"Of course," we said. "You know how some people are around here."

The real pay I received was a return of self-worth with the inestimable bonus of a greater appreciation for and understanding of "just folks" working for a living and making it. One of them was a senior bellman. He had done that work since his teen years. He never finished high school, yet was one of the most astute investors I've ever met, in addition to being a friend to many political and business leaders who frequented the hotel. By the time I was privileged to get to know him, he was in his 50s and had made enough money to put five children through college.

CHAPTER NINETEEN

MY LIFE WAS BECOMING RICH, CERTAINLY, not financially, but in ways beyond anything mere money could buy. Another example of how that worked was in my insurance man. He was a retired Marine Corps officer, and also someone who had stopped drinking years earlier. He readily shared his experiences with me. He introduced me to others who were, in the parlance of the day, "recovering alcoholics." Among Bob's advice to me was to insist I join the YMCA and start getting physically healthy again.

That I did, and the wondrous results of that advice are still with me today. Those words probably saved my life, actually. I was to experience a heart attack in 2001, but my recovery was very fast, and I'm still working out at the Y, encouraged by a group of cardiologists who promote eating right and staying physically fit. "I am most richly blessed," my friend Willy Steinbach often said, and I was to come to understand that as well.

Although touchy-feely happy talk blossomed all around me, there were still consequences. Ripples from splashes I had made long ago returned to me as waves to the shore. They would surprise me in ways like the poor captive cobra experienced, resting in his cool basket, when he hears the mellifluous flute and gracefully rises from the dark place into the light of day, only to be met by Ricki Ticki Tavi, a mongoose, one of the only animals fast enough to kill a cobra.

One day my mongoose shape-shifted into the Mother of all Consequences—the IRS found me.

It seems one of those letters I had incinerated while enjoying the spring sunlight of my new life, was a few choice *bon mots* from them. The IRS to me in that day was like the little kid's Closet Monster, a veritable house of horrors. My dereliction with the IRS was among the fearsome annoyances of life I had locked up in that mental vault I created years earlier to avoid bruising my over-blown self-image.

The IRS wanted a zillion dollars. They wanted it now, the letter said, or dire– *very dire*– consequences would follow. The letters were headed something like this:

NOTICE OF INTENT TO LEVY
Intent to seize your property or rights to property...
What you need to do immediately...

I think I had something like fifteen days to get it fixed.

My first reaction was to escape and evade again. Australia flashed through my mind. Better yet, how about Costa Rica? That got pretty popular with a couple of friends I had come to know. Before I could deploy my tactics, however, I had a new reaction, one that made much more sense than running. I thought to seek the advice of my friend and insurance man, Bob. Perhaps he had had some similar experience. I would go to him with this problem. What happened next would be one of the significant early milestones in my recovery.

I've never Bible-thumped, but I was versed in the Word of God. Somewhere in there, I think, is the thought that if a person who tries to do the right thing just does it, Satan will flee in disarray (always after a good try at derailing whatever "doing the right thing" was about). So filled with a new-found sense of hell-be-damned action, I overcame my irrational fears and false pride. I showed Bob what the IRS required of me.

"Great Gustifer" (as close to an epithet as he ever came) was his oh-so-encouraging response.

But then...

"That happened to me too." Magic words once more invoking the power of the shared experience.

"This is what I did," he said, leaning into his oaken desk piled high with phone messages, applications for insurance, policy abstracts and a Marine Corps KA-BAR combat knife for opening the mail... or something.

"Listen up. I know what you're thinking. You already told me about the Australia thing, you know. But running is the worst thing you could do. They will find you. The will win. And you must attack this problem now."

"With what? How?" I asked, looking at a certificate headed "Semper Fi" on his wall.

"How much money do you have right now?"

I told him. It wasn't much, but I was now getting a weekly pay check, at least. I could do something. "Always Faithful" began to stream on a parallel track in my mind as I felt my true character beginning its slow but determined comeback.

"Okay," Bob said. "Here what you do: Take $250 in cash. Go to the Post Office and get a money order for $250 made out to the U.S. Treasury– a money order. Don't write them a check because then they would know what account to seize if you screw this up."

"So that's it. That's what normal people do at times like this," I thought, amazed. "Then," Bob continued, and this really scared me , "take the money order to the IRS office in the Federal Building downtown."

"Into the valley of death rode the 600," immortal words from my high school English class attacked the synapses of my mind, but I also had a brief glimpse of the Brits and Aussies going over the top into sure death at Gallipoli.

"When you get there," Bob said, the look of a man of experience, "identify yourself and tell whoever you talk to that you owe the IRS some money and you want to pay them some of it right now and work something out on the balance."

Amazing, the logic...the rationality! I recalled I had once known such thinking. For a long time, in fact, it served me well. Here it was back again.

I did it. I marched myself downtown, right into the Valley of the Shadow of Death, while "cannon to the left of me, cannon to the right of me volleyed and thundered." Yes, I soldiered on and went to the IRS.

The experience's great epiphany was that this new way of life I was now negotiating made reality easier to handle. The way I dealt with this crisis *du jour*– and the others which were inevitable– made me feel better, and in my romantic way of thinking, my attitude once more evoked The Godfather. When the five New York families went to war they "went to the mattresses," places of focus, protection and defense. I joined them in my mind.

I was sober but still a little nuts, a well-disguised whack-job. The years of alcohol abuse still affected me. I knew it would take time, and much hard work would be necessary for this reprieve from the zombie life I had seemed hell-bent on. With focus, hard work and good folks watching my back, I knew that was the truth.

Looking back, I am astounded at how horrified I had been at such a straight-forward approach to my tax problem. Millions of others have them all the time, but this was the first time I had actually confronted mine. I had seen the closet door bulging menacingly. My every nerve ending crackled with a strange new energy.

Little did I know but that odd feeling, a distinctive nervous energy, was suppressed by years awash in alcohol, and that new energy was to power my recovery from then on.

The man I met behind the desk at the IRS was friendly and open. The pure-government-issue office– bland walls papered with posters of instructions on how to get more instructions, a few cheap armless plastic seats all in a section that a guy in a uniform watched– was where I needed to be.

The man at the desk, a youngish "boy next door" type in a blue-striped tie, heard me out, accepted the money order and thanked me for coming in. He assured me that "we could work something out." Then he told me something amazing that I had not thought of before.

"Looking at your account, Mr. Blue"– he was scrutinizing a computer terminal before him– "your situation is not really so bad. I have to chase people down all day for amounts ten times or more than this. I'm glad you came in. Not many people do."

So it came to be that I grasped my first lesson in the power of redemption. No longer just an intellectual concept, now it had legs. So did Satan. The dust flew, as he fled in disarray.

No more would I see the mocking rictus of a Lesser Simian slapping the ground in front of me with a macabre grin. I did not let rumbles from the past get me off-track. I became an expert at one thing and one thing only– recovery. Soon I had literally hundreds of new friends– all of whom I met while trudging that path– a walk many have taken– and most of them even today among my best friends ever.

Then came a wondrous day– the day that I was able to celebrate a big victory in my new found life: nine months of continuous sobriety.

I celebrated appropriately... about eight cups of high-test coffee and hundreds of calories of cake. The combination will make you feel a little high, by the way, but I never wrapped my car around a light pole under the influence of caffeine and sugar– the consequence of that would come later through a little book called *Sugar Blues* which roared through the recovery community like a prairie fire in the days to come.[24]

At this celebratory point, the yang of the time happened. While I had lost the job I walked out of earlier and had gone to work for the hotel, there was still something looming in the gloom just offstage. Here was a real irony. I had turned a defeat into victory. I had completed something significant, instead of jumping down the rabbit hole again. Yet there was something else out there... something bigger, something that could have thrown me back to the place where yet the Luger lay.

CHAPTER TWENTY

IRONY IS JUST AN INTELLECTUAL CONCEPT compared with a broken heart.

Irony lay in circumstances of getting my life back together without benefit of a mind-altering drug– the one that had told me, as Bluto philosophized in *Animal House* when a "brother" faced adversity: "My advice to you is to begin drinking heavily."

Now a new irony lay in my path, while heartbreak hid in the ditches of its emotional border hedges. I stumbled into them with the realization that my children were being hidden from me.

The kind of direct action that I had learned when I overcame my fears of the IRS– accompanied by rigorous self-honesty– would soon map my course in dealing with the more complex issue of my kids. My ex and her boyfriend remained elusive. Neither my mother-in-law nor my friend Bob, who was something of an amateur sleuth, was able to find them. It became obvious they were hiding a secret.

Once I understood that, I realized my soon-to-be-ex-wife (it took a year in Virginia from filing to a final divorce decree in those days) and her male companion were hiding from me... from us, all of my allies, her mother included. I was pretty anxious, not over her whereabouts, but for my children's welfare. Anxiety turned to anger and fear. The counselors in the relevant juvenile and domestic relations court were insensitive to my plight. In fact, I learned about institutionalized anti-male bias concerning children during those days– the mid-70s.

The government apparatchiks in their domestic-relations bunkers, shielded by the imprimatur of the courts, worked under the apparent assumption that the father was most likely wrong in child visitation and custody matters— especially fathers with an admitted history of alcohol abuse. The latter point I accepted. They were right. I needed time to prove myself. My lawyer told me the same thing. So I accepted the facts as they were, but I would not relent on seeing my kids. The stone wall of discrimination stood in my way, not by overt actions, but by inaction. I would wait them out, and then turn inaction against the system's sycophants.

"Be the best Doug you can be," Bob said. I would wait until I had a year of sobriety before attacking the problem; meanwhile I would keep doing my best to stabilize my life. I had no idea if that approach would work or not. The walk became one of faith.

Little did I guess, however, that when the time came, I would upset the established applecart with élan and cause a courtroom show that not only did other lawyers come in to see but which would be worthy of a whole season of "Judge Judy" boiled down to about ten minutes.

Time does indeed wound all heels.

I became an expert at learning my new way of life, an expert at living a day at a time, without benefit of anything psychotropic (unless you could call caffeine that), and being the best at sobriety that I could be.

That included helping others, of course, which I did when asked. Once I was at a coffee-house hangout for recoverees, and the self-appointed major-domo of the group asked me if I would drive a guy to the Medical College of Virginia's Alcoholism Treatment Unit. I readily agreed.

He was a small, disheveled guy. His thinning brown hair needed a trim, and he smoked a lot, always holding his cigarette with that slight palsy I recognized so well. But I sensed he was good inside, sincere and deserved a abreak. He deserved the chance to make it. So we rolled.

On the way there— a good twenty or so blocks of downtown traffic away— I tried to make small talk with the poor fellow, but about all he could manage to say stopped me cold.

"I'm just really worried," he said.

"About what?" I asked. "They'll take good care of you, and I guarantee that if you get with their program, you'll be out here with the rest of us recovering drunks learning how to have a real life."

"Yeah, but I might not even make it down there," he said.

"Why?"

"Because I keep having them damned seizures."

I'm sure my eyes widened as I flashed back to my experience of seeing an alcoholic seizure in Newport News, and the possibility that a seizure could kill. I began to look for a police car, or at least a place to pull out of traffic and get some help with this guy (the time being the dark age before cellular phones).

I saw neither policeman nor a place to pull over safely, so we kept moving forward in the stop-and-go traffic and made it to the hospital without incident. He was admitted. I breathed a sigh of relief, reminded again of the tests life brings. They always move us along to the next plateau. I began to ask myself "What next?"

Soon after that, approaching sobriety's one-year mark, it was time to find my kids. My lawyer and I went back to court to seek enforcement of the separation agreement's visitation clause. I wanted to see my kids again. My ex's time was up. The Juvenile and Domestic Relations Court agreed with us, ordered monthly visitations to begin and told us where my ex and the kids were.

For the initial visitation, my friend Tommy went with me because I figured I might need a witness. A well-dressed, Yale-educated business executive, he added credibility to my mission, and backup. We showed up right on time on the day the Court had appointed. The place was a small, well-kept apartment complex just north of Richmond's city limits. But the first visitation was a non-starter. My ex cracked the door and said the kids were "sick" and did not want to go with me anyway. I could not even get a look to see if they were even there.

The following month, I tried again and this time the kids went with me. However, I sensed their tension. I noticed their lack of eye contact with me. They had been set-up, and so had I. We got to the sidewalk in front of the apartment, and, as if on cue, the kids took off. They ran around behind the apartment building. That way they could re-enter the apartment through the back door, where I'm convinced my ex waited, betting I would not try to follow. She was right. I stayed where Tommy could see it all.

This scene was duplicated the following month. That was enough.

Obviously the kids had been instructed in what I saw as a rather amateurish evasive tactic, perhaps even a goad to get me to force the issue and do something stupid. But stupid, I'm not. I had done the night police beat as a daily newspaper reporter. I had seen the havoc and violence that sometimes resulted in similar situations. "Domestics," the police called them.

So, my ex had just blown her chances to be reasonable, and, as I had promised myself at a year of sobriety, it was time to go back to court and force this issue the correct way. We had won easily in the lower court, but my ex made the mistake of appealing. The next level would be a hearing in the jurisdiction's Circuit Court, in Virginia, a court-of-record. It would be a bigger deal, well above the pettifoggery of the bureaucracy.

Much grander than the smaller lower court, the Circuit Court bore the imprimatur of much more serious judicial authority. My lawyer Frank and I were at a table before the bar on the left, my ex– now on her second lawyer– on the right. The court's clerk emerged through a rear door and bade us "all rise." The black-robed Circuit Court judge entered. After he was seated, the case was announced by another clerk and a court reporter began to record the proceeding.

The basic facts were established, the separation agreement, the lower court's ruling, the failure of the monthly visitations the agreement clearly called for. The rest was pretty simple and short. The judge sternly ordered compliance with the visitation provisions that the lower court had ordered. He set a second date to hear that it had been accomplished. And he made it quite clear that he did not suffer gladly taking his docket's time on something as clear cut and obvious.

Once more with Tommy as back up and witness, visitation met the same cheap duplicity as before. So it was back to court again. Only this time, the stakes would be higher, the consequences, dire.

This time, when the judge entered the courtroom, he was clearly unhappy. Under oath I told my side of the story, which I did thoroughly. Cross examination was a joke. The opposing lawyer was an old courthouse relic. He couldn't see well, and when he found out he wasn't going to get anywhere with me, he then made a classic mistake by asking his client to take the stand. My lawyer winked at me, a smile hinted.

Frank was a big guy, an expert competitive pistol marksman with deep trial experience. He could be intimidating when he needed to be. He started off all smiles, ingratiatingly asking mild and innocuous basic stuff: "Please state your full name... and were you born and raised here in Richmond?... and were you in fact married to my client... how many children did you have with him... and what are their names...".... and la-dee-dah until the peace and serenity was so thick somnolence was just another question away. But then the hammer fell.

"Do you have any other children than the two by my client?"

She did, of course, pregnancy being rather hard to hide. And that was the secret that had caused them to escape and evade us all those months. It ruined her whole case, not to mention the credibility any mother should be accorded. She had become pregnant with the child of another while still legally married to me. But perhaps a bigger mistake was her response to the court:

"I do not have to answer that question."

I thought the judge was going to leap over the bar and throttle her. There followed a dramatic, harsh and basic lecture on what witnesses can do and cannot do in his court– "a Court of Record," he reminded us all.

He ordered a ten-minute recess. When we reconvened, the judge reentered, his look one a defendant would never want to see. The courtroom was heavy with anticipation. All eyes were on the judge, and not a sound was heard except the swooshing of his robes as he seated himself. The atmosphere was charged. Nobody moved.

Once settled, he scanned his domain, a claque of visiting lawyers riveted on the back row. The judge's instructions were quite clear. He ordered one more try at a successful visitation. I was to come back in thirty days and report the results. If it failed, my ex– my children's mother– would be back in his court to answer why she should not be held in contempt of court and sentenced to thirty days in jail. BAM went the gavel. Court was adjourned.

Unbelievably, the visitation failed again. Another stupid evasive move, similar to those that had gone before, was forced on my children. To this day I do not understand why someone in authority could not or would not have recognized this behavior as child-abuse. Realistically, however, this was happening in 1976. Things would change, but not that year. So maybe I was a pioneer of sorts because when we went back to court, several of my lawyer friends were there again to see what would happen, for I was in an unusual position: I held the power of my testimony to send a my ex to jail.

I was going to do it, too.

Anger drove that decision. When I walked into the courthouse that day, I was fed up. It had been much more than a year since I'd had meaningful time with my children. I was outraged by a system whose first-line functionaries offered not a scintilla of help or sympathy. I was grateful to the law and my lawyer, but enough was enough.

"Frank, I'm going to do it," I said.

"It's your call to make," he said. "The judge would really appreciate a compromise, though."

Once we were in the waiting area on the second floor of the courts building, us on one side, them on the other, waiting for a previous case to be heard, Frank once again asked me to consider compromise.

"No way," I said. Then the other side's lawyer approached. He was new, and approached me with a weasley attitude. He asked me to compromise, too.

"Get lost," I said.

Wisely, he did. Then I turned away, and out of lip-reading range, said: "What will happen, Frank, if I simply tell the truth in there?"

"After the judge hears your account," he said, also covering his mouth, "he will probably order a thirty-day conviction for contempt of court to be served on consecutive weekends."

"So she really would do the time..." I thought of my kids. Then I knew what I had to do. But I let things simmer. The minutes seemed to drag to a near dead-stop as I willed the tension to escalate, the drama to build. I would wait until the absolute last second. I was going to send an unmistakable and unforgettable message. Time crawled. I crossed my arms in front of me and just stood there, facing the court's closed doors, awaiting their beckon. Feet planted an aggressive foot apart, glowering like Clint Eastwood about to make someone's day, I waited for my moment.

As the doors opened and the people from the preceding case left, a court official called ours. Just before we walked into the courtroom, I said:

"Frank, tell the judge I will compromise. I cannot let my kids see their mother go to jail."

He was visibly relieved.

"Good call. I knew you would make it. Thanks."

I was relieved, too. Plus I knew I had made my point. My dabbling in drama as a teenager proved my able ally, but I had learned something very important: "Always examine your motives first," someone once told me. "That is a part of a successful life in recovery." Then I thought about my angel. She was there that day. And we would meet again soon.

PART SIX

Death and the Angel

CHAPTER TWENTY-ONE

KICKING THE -ISM DOWN THE ROAD IS DEADLY. Some folks in recovery use "ism" as shorthand for the all-too-common failure to make right the wrongs of the past by disconnecting -ism from alcohol. But if it's connected– alcohol-ism– getting it right first can make the difference between successful recovery or failure. The -ism is an incomplete job, prone to fall apart in the storms of life that always come. Or the unwillingness to participate fully with the "recovering community"– helping others to find their way. Denying the -ism means carrying on as though nothing bad had really happened.

It did, of course. Denial shrouds that fact. But those who recognize -ism's reality will find an enlightened path. On it they will find the power of the shared experience. That power cuts two ways, because there are always those who cannot abide change, or they may not believe it possible, in fact.

When I first read Bill Wilson's comment about "profound personality change," I admit I felt push-back, my own resistance to change. That reaction stemmed from something I had somehow absorbed growing up. It was a tired old Southern dogma wrapped up in lemmas like "You can't teach an old dog new tricks." But we can change. The collective experience of successful recovery by millions world-wide proves that. It is not a theory but a necessity for a successful recovery and life.

Recently I watched a short YouTube video a friend sent me. It was a powerful testimony from one of our nation's high-profile political leaders. This time, he was not running for anything. He spoke from the heart about his own experience growing up. There were problems– most of them familiar to most of us, if we care to look. The most dramatic part of what this leader had to say was that he turned to the book *Alcoholic Anonymous*, the famous "big book," for help. He had access to it because of his grandmother, who had helped raise him. She had been sober in AA for more than thirty years. Not having an alcohol problem himself, nevertheless, he read her book and took from it the "What" I've been talking about– the profound power of the shared experience– what we did. In his case, it was encapsulated in the principles of AA's Twelve Steps.[25] They changed his life and reinforced his belief in a God who loves us and intervenes for us daily, not just the one he had learned about in Sunday School and church. They can sometimes be quite different, as I was soon to discover.

It started in the room where the ruling court of one of my former churches met– well appointed, but not over-the-top. Presbyterian, in other words, like a traditional corporate boardroom with paintings of Nineteenth Century men on horses on walls of light Williamsburg taupe. It would end with dramatic proof of the truth behind Plato's aphorism about "the unexamined life."

Well into successful sobriety by then, I had many friends in that church, including some who had experienced the tragedy of losing loved ones to drug overdoses and the chaos that alcohol abuse can wreak. Those tragedies had led the church to form a mechanism to help others to prevent or learn how to deal with such problems. I had been asked to come and speak to a personnel issue at the heart of that mechanism. The clergy were supportive of the principles of recovery necessary to a new life. They embraced the disease concept of chemical dependency, as did most of the staff and lay leadership. But I soon learned that not all did, and all was not as it seemed. Enmity lay within.

A minority of the governing board I was meeting with had successful experiences with recovery. Most, however, seemed not to have had direct experience with chemical dependency or were simply in denial.

The room may have been typical of most church boards of its time, but that day its mood was not. A modern-day suburban Protestant Inquisition looks like a gray-business-suited corporate board of directors debating how to ax an employee who has been hand-picked for the job of standing in the gap between them— the ruling establishment— and the myriad of alcohol and drug problems and accompanying dysfunctions that will happen in a congregation in the four digits.

The inquisition was not about me but a close friend, a counselor, one with many years of successful experience employed by the church. The question on the table ostensibly concerned the counselor's compensation. However, for a few it was the counselor's very presence on staff that was their problem. Things were getting a little too close for comfort for some. So the crypto-agenda was that some wanted this highly professional and credentialed person out.

My job was to support my friend, as I had been asked to do, and urge the board to retain the position of in-house mental health counselor on staff. I decided the best way to do this was to share my own experience with recovery and explain the vital role professional counseling had played in it. So I did that as forthrightly as I could. I minced no words, played no politics and backed up what I said with stats and studies.

As I spoke, I watched my audience closely. Body language spoke back. Some sat tight-faced with arms crossing their chests. They were the Pharisees. Others smiled and nodded encouragement to me as I spoke. They were the Disciples. But most were corporate-stoic. That was not unusual. I'd been on those boards, too, in the past, and that was the way you did it. Just like the big businesses downtown or the poker players across town. On the margins, however, a few seemed receptive to my message, a few were not. In fact they were downright uncomfortable. I saw fear in two. Their eyes gave them away. I later felt the anger of one in particular.

Whether in meetings, classes, socials, or just in passing, that individual and I always had been on friendly terms. After this gathering, however, his reaction to me was as if I no longer existed, complete ostracism with never another word. His behavior reflected an extremity of behavior I have noticed only a few times over the years. Whenever I or anyone else speaks to a general audience quite frankly about the ills that alcohol or other drugs can wreak, bad reactions by a few are likely. They are a dead giveaway of skeletons in the closet, simians in the living room. And they cannot hide.

How do I know that? Personal experience. I exhibited the same behavior in my pathless darker days. I once worked around a big, friendly, gregarious guy who never knew a cranky moment. He was open about his "new life" sober in AA. I hated him. He was happy. I was not, because I knew my closet needed cleaning and my living room was carpeted with eggshells.

CHAPTER TWENTY-TWO

BY THE LATE 70s, THE ONCE-FASHIONABLE intersection of Harrison and Grace Streets in mid-town Richmond had deteriorated. In its high-life during the first half of the last century, its classic Georgian and Federalist facades graced a predominantly residential area bracketed by small businesses, restaurants, an old-school hospital, a big stone church and the incunabulum of a huge university.

But by that spring day in 1977, the corner had become a city planner's nightmare. Its northwestern quadrant once hosted the dignified St. Luke's Hospital, the place where I was born. By that day, however, the classic stone exterior and dark wood interior had been knocked down for a parking lot, now populated more by weeds and untrimmed grass than cars. But it was still a fashionable spot... for derelicts.

My experience there added a new chapter to my never-ending liberal arts education— yes, another Lesser Simian, but as I was beginning to learn, not fearsome but one which held another lesson. It showed me how dramatic could be the fall from grace of those who were hooked on alcohol— and would not or could not get off— or who had gone frighteningly beyond the point where they even could: the point of no return.

That day I was pretty down in the dumps— issues still dangled, stability tantalized just beyond reach, and a girlfriend had just dumped me. So I called my old friend Tommy. He had been around recovery for a long time. He understood where I was.

"Come on by," he said.

The tired, modest, 50s-neo-modernist look of his office building belied its interior. Tommy sat behind a dark-wooded executive desk amongst expensive accoutrements on what appeared to be a costly oriental rug, dark in tone to match the gravitas of his position.

"Don't sit," he said as soon as I walked in, "we're going for a little ride."

Just a few blocks west on the corner that had once hosted the hospital, a worn stone balustrade was all that was left of St. Luke's. Perched there like three old crows were three old men, or at least they looked old. They were street people, and each clutched his brown bag. Tommy had brought me to this place to meet one of them, Chesley.

"Hi, Tommy," the one called Chesley said.

"Are you in or out?" Tommy said.

"I'm out. They kicked me out" he said, referring to the AA clubhouse a few blocks to the east.

"But it's good to see you, Tommy."

"Well, I'm just glad to see you're still vertical."

A crack broke across the wrinkles of Chesley's sun-reddened granite-like face. It could have been a smile.

Tommy introduced me as a friend. I sat down with Chesley, and he started.

"I tried to get straight but just couldn't make it past a few weeks at most," he said.

I listened. That, plus being Tommy's friend is how I gained his trust, I believe. Chesley told me his story, one that made me feel grateful to hear for what I heard was a saga so sad it chilled me even in the sun of a high-summer's day.

He spoke in a low, measured, articulate monotone.

Chesley had graduated from the United States Military Academy at West Point. He went on to an Army career from which he retired as a full colonel. And no "drunk talk" was this, for Tommy had known him for years and had confirmed his background. I was there that morning to hear this story.

After retiring, Chesley recalled, he proceeded to drink to his present state. He lost everything, including his family. They let him go. They'd probably done all they thought they could. All he had was a military pension. Sometimes it showed up at a local homeless agency; sometimes not. He wasn't sure where it was going since he'd left the homeless shelter because they did not allow drinking. He had no real address. The spaces under bridges are on no one's postal route.

Chesley's message was that if you have the chance to recover, the opportunity to get well, even a slight slim chance of a better life, take it. There might not be another.

If you don't take it, your life can be just like his, which appeared to me to be a one-way street by then.

I shared my story with him. We connected, and when I felt the moment had come, I asked him if he'd like to try again. Alcoholism is no respecter of age, nor is sobriety. He was so obviously intelligent, certainly he could understand that "second chances" can happen more than just twice.

"I tried AA several times and failed," he said. "I showed up drunk enough times so that they kept kicking me out. Then I was banned from that place called 'the club' up the street."

"Let's go talk to the house manager." I meant Tommy and me. "They'll listen to us. And it's been a while, so we could probably get you another chance," I said.

By then, Chesley's drinking buddies had heard enough. They took off. And at just about the same time, Chesley said, "Yeah, maybe I will try again."

A subtle lightening, a slight lessening of the tensions of years seemed to cross Chesley's weather-beaten old face. Was that hope? Or was it just wishful thinking on my part? Whatever it was seemed to reflect a hint that somebody gave a damn, after all. I caught it and felt better. We agreed to help him try again.

Tommy and I went back to his office and then went to have lunch. There he showed me that exercise was just as much for Chesley as it was for me. Sharing with another, with whom I shared the common bond of alcoholism, was what I needed to get over my funk. It worked. I'd forgotten about it. Helping others is the way we help ourselves and that's why you hear people say recovery is "a selfish" process. Yes, but

163

not as the world thinks of selfish, one-sided; but selfish in another dimension, a multi-sided win-win proposition.

Chesley was going to meet me at the front door of "the Club" at noon Thursday, two days away.

The day came, and I was out on the sidewalk in the hot summer sun waiting for him. The building that served as the meeting place was an old two-story brick structure, a small business many years earlier. Inside was like a meeting of a tobacco workers' union: less oxygen than carbon dioxide, carbon monoxide, gaseous sulfuric acid and whatever else there is in cigarette smoke.

The first floor was a general meeting room. All sorts of people were usually hanging out, from street people to millionaires, people driving twenty-year-old Plymouths and those driving brand-new Cadillacs– all kinds, but all sharing one thing: they worked to find and maintain sobriety in the lifelong process of recovery. Thousands have been helped there since its establishment– a gift from a grateful businessman who had donated the building years earlier.

At the end of the first-floor open area was a real bar, a wood-hewn original, except now it was a coffee bar, with a bartender. His name was Bob. Bob was pretty much a permanent fixture, although he claimed to "have a little business on the side." He once offered me a job there.

"You got a car, right?" he asked.

"Yeah, why?"

"I can set you up with me in a business that can make you $400 a week."

"Doing what?"

"Escort service. Easy work. Here's my card. Call me if you're interested." Bob left it at that.

"AA Outcall Massage Service," the card said, along with a phone number.

I seriously thought about it because I needed the money. But the thought only lasted about forty-five seconds, which was about forty seconds too long after "pimp" came to mind. I did not dress the part and wasn't about to put a faux-gold grill on my Chevrolet.

The second-floor of the Club was a meeting room with a rostrum and podium for speakers who would share their stories in meetings. On the wall behind the speakers' rostrum hung a framed yard-sale apotheosis of Jesus Christ as a paragon of white northern European extraction– the same non-Semitic romanticism I've seen in certain churches.

The building was on a side street between major in-town thoroughfares. The only thing on the door indicating what it was were the numbers "210." So there I waited in the hot sun for Chesley to come 'round the corner any minute. The meeting started at noon. But by then there was no Chesley, nor was there ten minutes later. Or ever. We got word Chesley died a few days after that. Alcohol poisoning.

CHAPTER TWENTY-THREE

AT ABOUT THREE AND A HALF YEARS SOBER, I was doing well in recovery. Then I wasn't– like sailing across a placid bay into a sudden summer storm when through the fog you see a hulking form bearing down on you. The waves of early recovery can be like that.

My sobriety was intact, but my worldly affairs were falling apart. I had blundered into another entrepreneurial venture that cycled in and out of the real world like a shooting star. Once more, money became a problem. Bills late, child support a struggle, rent a dance with imminent eviction. I was a mess in the eyes of the Earth People. And my thinking– remember, still affected by the years of pickling– took a giant step backwards. Once more the same mechanism that had once led to suicidal ideation kicked in. Only this time, death wasn't the objective. It was all wrapped up in thinking that life was better when I was drinking.

Because, I told myself, when I was drinking my thinking was more creative. I was more resourceful– so much so that I could leap tall circumstances in a single bound and land in a new place every time. Drinking drove that process. So shouldn't I just say to hell with this "recovery" stuff? I did better back then. Like the ancient Israelites, tired of that Moses guy leading them in circles around the desert, I wanted to go back to Egypt.

But the folks I trusted most in the world, a close-knit group of guys in recovery, most of them well ahead of me, guys who knew no secrets from each other– reminded me, again, "When the going gets tough, the tough get going." In the process, I found my own Moses.

"Why don't you go and talk with Dr. Hoff?" one suggested.

He referred to Dr. Ebbe Curtis Hoff, a pioneer in the treatment of chemical dependency, a man with an outsized heart and a world-class intellect. I had met him along the path of recovery.

After World War II, in which he had served in the U.S. Navy as a flight surgeon and as Naval Attaché to The Court of St. James's, London, Dr. Hoff moved to Virginia where he founded and led one of the nation's first state agencies focused on substance abuse issues. He also chaired the Department of Neurological Sciences at the Medical College of Virginia and became a great friend of the recovery community throughout the state, speaking regularly before groups and always an open, friendly and wise counselor, advisor and encourager to individuals within that movement.[26]
When I called, he remembered me.

I told him my thinking was slipping into depression and I needed some help with it. He wanted to know how, exactly, I knew that. I told him:

I couldn't sleep, had begun to isolate, felt nothing was working out, jumped around in my thinking. I was inconsistent in making decisions, constantly worried about money and sometimes felt like my life was going nowhere and I would never get much better. I had begun to question whether life was worth living.

As soon as I said it, that last point shocked me. It came from the darkest depths of my being, places that were closed for business. But it was true. And I said it. Like sending up a search flare on a Moon-less star-less night, it cried "Help."

Dr. Hoff and I began to meet each week and, with improvement, would meet once or twice a month. He agreed to put me on a sliding scale related to how much money I was making, which was not very much. It was a gift from God, for here was the man who probably did more in his time to advance thinking and public policy about alcoholism in Virginia in the mid-twentieth century than anyone else.

He is perhaps best known for his straightforward advocacy of treating alcoholism as a medical condition and not a moral failing. Among his many books, *Alcoholism: The Hidden Disease*, continues to be instructive to both professionals as well as the general public. Needless to say, I began to learn a great deal.

First, my brand of depression could be comprehended. I could see it, feel it, identify it. I learned its triggers and its boundaries, when and why it started and ended. It was episodic. During the periods between down times, I began to learn which behaviors were triggers, and to distinguish them from those which were helpful. Dr. Hoff was teaching me how to find my own way out.

I began to see my own depression as unreal. I could not produce a half-pound of it and put it on an examination table. By imaging it this way, I felt I had power over it, not vice-versa. Rather, it was in my head alone. I would deal with it there, on my terms, and separate it from my thoughts and actions to the extent possible. I learned about, studied and practiced cognitive behavior therapy. Over time what I learned worked wonders to restore me to the place in the world where the Earth People lived, owned houses, drove new cars, provided for their families and paid their bills. An amazing transformation had begun, and I knew that.

It was not like my fallen-from-grace West Point Colonel said it was. But it was very intense– tough– one of the most difficult times of my life. My family, yet leery, I could feel that. Old friends, some still tentative and wearing wary looks when they saw me but no longer crossing the street when they saw me coming. I mean, there was that. A glimmer of progress. At the height of this intense time, I experienced something that I cannot explain but which would forever change me.

Dr. Hoff's office was in one of the megaliths that made up the Medical College of Virginia campus in downtown Richmond. Today it is known as the Virginia Commonwealth University Medical Center, and its growing number of big buildings continues to overwhelm icons of the city's historic past.

The White House of the Confederacy, the home of its president, Jefferson Davis, sits in the midst of all this high-rise high-tech health care, beside the central site of the Museum of the Confederacy. Two blocks west lie rows of classic 19th

Century homes, where history had been made from the city's earliest days, where hauntings were whispered of and espionage blossomed during the Civil War.

In the midst of this curious dichotomy of history and modernist medical eminence, I would get a cup of coffee at a restaurant called "The Skull and Bones," before my appointments with Dr. Hoff.

I would take my coffee up the red-bricked sidewalk to a bench in front of the Valentine–Wickham house in the 1000 block of East Clay Street in an area known as Court End, a popular tourist destination. Its quiet tree-shaded repose coexisted with the freneticism of advanced learning. A curious mix of driven students, dedicated teachers, nervous patients and families joined bus-loads of bug-eyed, camera-toting visitors, their touristy marsupial pouches propped upon prosperous American paunches.

I would sit on my bench under a canopy of live oaks just a few yards from the center of Confederate rodomontade and make notes in my ever–present notebook, awaiting my time with Dr. Hoff.

One day, the sun of high-summer shimmered through the trees, and the birds sang liltingly, while I– in this island of genteel tranquility– felt terrible. The now familiar litany of stuff that was wrong with my life ran like a steroid-powered slideshow through my head. I began to feel hopeless and very tired of what I was beginning to see as an unending struggle. And at just that point– the perfect point– I heard a woman say: "Everything's going to be all right now, Doug."

It was an audible voice. But there was no one there. It was between class-changes, and no tourists lingered outside the museums at either end of Court End. No humans, anyway, but a clarion voice, just as audible as that of someone in a room with me. Stupefied, I did all I knew to do. I wrote it down, without a clue as to what was really happening. Before it dawned on me that I might be mad or hallucinating, I realized that it was time for my appointment with Dr. Hoff.

I was grateful that I had come to know Dr. Hoff as a serious Christian. He and his wife Phebe were very active in the Episcopal Church and now lie in serene repose in a grove of trees surrounding St. Mary's Episcopal Church just west of Richmond not far from Tuckahoe, the plantation where Thomas Jefferson spent his boyhood years. I have been to St. Mary's to commune with them.

"An outstanding quality of Dr. Hoff, which is apparent to all who come into contact with him," wrote Dr. Frank A. Sexias, medical director of the National Council on Alcoholism in 1974, "is his deep and abiding religious faith which appears to inform his every action." [27]

Dr. Hoff spoke often to me of the power of God to help me help myself to heal and find the sweet-spot of long-term recovery. And so when I went in to his office, welcomed by his friendly countenance, I immediately told him what had just happened to me.

His reaction was equally immediate:

"That was clearly an angel, Dougald." (He preferred the Scottish fullness of my first name over the Americanized version.)

His tone was one of expectation, almost as if he knew this would come to pass. His understanding of the spiritual component of recovery was well known to many of us in our community. His quick response resonated with me, a lifelong– albeit seriously back-slid– believer. Next came his very clear instructions. He said this marked a turning point in my struggle. He said we did not really need to meet that day, but instead he asked me to go and reflect on the moment.

"I want you to write down everything that happens to you over the next several days," he said, "and then come back to see me in two weeks and tell me what happened."

And our meeting was over.

I left with the most curious confluence of exuberance and fear I had ever experienced. Things were to change, and I knew it.

My trips to see Dr. Hoff became rituals. I enjoyed the process, for it gave me something solid, predictable and helpful to do in a time of frightening disarray.

Simultaneously a good friend who owned a small ad agency had invited me to use office space in his business.

"Use this office," Jim said. It was up front just behind his receptionist's space next to the front door. "Make calls, send out resumes, whatever you need to do."

The neighborhood around Jim's office building centered on Second and East Cary Streets. An open and supportive business enclave radiated outward from there, a multi-talented concentration of creative buzz. With its eclectic mix of architectural styles– brownstones, old townhomes, attractive Federalist rows and the occasional modernist intrusion– the area contrasted with the so-called "central business district" six or eight blocks or so down the hill, the main part of downtown Richmond. There rose sleek high rises with their invisible, unknowable inhabitants, hiding behind one-way windows as if to say, "We can see you but you can't see us." The feel of the new developers' dream downtown and its towers of anonymity was one of exclusion.

But the enclave– the creative ghetto of The Day– was a matrix of ad agencies and PR firms, their courtesans, supplicants and suppliers– artists, photographers, type salesmen, printing reps, modeling agencies, filmmakers and writers. They formed an open, funky, supportive counterpoint to their neighbors down the hill. They were an informal community which would, of course, presage the core of the old city's manifest destiny as a center for the creative arts.

So I settled in to the ghetto– even wrote a few press releases for a couple of Jim's clients– and I made my calls. I was pretty connected actually, and contrary to what my sometimes negative self-talk said, I discovered a network I could activate.

The creative neighborhood, became action central after my angelic visitation. Something amazing was supposed to take place there, I thought. But my notes– the ones I told Dr. Hoff I would write about what happened to me, were turning out to be dull and routine. There's only so much you can write about hot, humid Southern summer days with folks walking around exuding creativity. I began to wonder if my now-suspect brain chemicals were playing some sick game with me until one day at lunch at the restaurant diagonally across the street– the one habituated by the creative class— a friend stopped me and said, "Say, Doug did you know Pauline had left the TV station?"

"No, I didn't. Who's taking her place?" I asked, seeing this as just more of the routine community gossip, people playing the scene while being seen.

"Well... I thought you might want to call them." He said, a facial query forming,"... in case you might be interested."

"Maybe so," said I to myself as the Mad Hatter whispered in my ear.

"Thanks for passing that along."

I blew the thought out of mind. I didn't think I was qualified for that. The job was public relations director for our local Public Broadcasting affiliates. I had worked with them as a corporate supporter in the bad days— the drinking days, the times when I didn't necessarily remember everything, like where I had left the company car, whom I had befriended... or insulted. A healthful sense of self-worth was not with me that day.

But when the phone rang a couple of days later and someone I had not seen in years, a person who would not have known of my earlier contact about Pauline's job, called and suggested I talk to them about it, some of my nerves' lights clicked to green. That got my attention, but I did not do anything about it then either.

When it happened a third time— again from a person who would not have known either of the other two— I sat bolt upright. There's something about things that happen in threes, and "threes" scare Mad Hatters. So this time, I recalled what people had been telling me for a long time: "Go for it. What have you got to lose?"

I went for it, to the top.

I had met the founder, chairman and CEO of the organization years earlier at a cocktail party. Smiling at the irony, I recalled the party. It celebrated the funding for Public Broadcasting of an unusual telecast— a drama written by an inmate of the Virginia State Penitentiary, in those days a baleful yet classically proportioned presence just between the edges of Richmond's downtown business community and the James River. Its core structure had been designed by Thomas Jefferson.

While the Pen's outside was interesting and historic, its inside was sinister and threatening. Working on the television program, I got to go there three times. "The Dark Side it was," would Yoda have said.

After passing through a reception area, an armed guard escorted me through a door to a very plain grey area. No carpet, nothing on the concrete walls, and only one way to go– behind bars.

I was directed to enter a smallish area through a sliding barred floor-to-ceiling gate. It slammed shut as soon as I was in. The only way out was its twin at the other end, and that slammed shut, too. I heard heavy locks clank into place. I thought of making some comment, like: "So that's why they call it the slammer, huh?" but bit my tongue.

This was the holding cell where I gave up my wallet and keys, but I got to keep my belt, pen and notebook.

Once inside, a couple of guards met me. They led me down a plain gray corridor opening onto a large and long cellblock. As we walked through it, I flashed back to the movie *Stir Crazy*. In a classic scene, Gene Wilder and Richard Pryor are walking through a cellblock, and Pryor is trying to teach Wilder how to walk– to do the urban-pimp-roll– like a veteran inmate into The Place, detainees hooting and clanging their cell bars.

"Yeah, we bad!" Pryor tells Wilder to say. Wilder squeaks it out. It could have been filmed in this cellblock, three tiers of misery in cells of steel with walls of stone magnifying the slightest of sounds.

We made our way through the cellblock to a theater where I met the young man who had penned the play. The cast was rehearsing. They were really a wonderful troupe, excited about the project and its prospects as a TV production. The lead was an older man. I asked him why he was there.

"Oh... well, murder-one, actually," he said. Just another day on the set.

The show went on to production, and I returned to the State Pen two more times, once with a rather comely drama critic for one of the local newspapers.

Our long walk through the cellblock– she attired in a rather tight-fitting skirt– trumped the Pryor-Wilder show by a country mile.

The televised play was a huge success, celebrated with a lavish cocktail party. That memory informed my next move, and that's why I knew I had nothing to lose and everything to gain that morning.

I called the TV station's chairman and CEO directly, briefly re-introduced myself and told him why I was calling. He said– in his West Texas broadcast-engineer drawl–

"Sure, Doug, I remember you. Why don't you come on down to see me?"

"Thanks, I'd like to do that. What day would be convenient for you?"

"Heck, I don't know. Why don't you come on down here right now?"

I did. And after some small talk, he said, "So what can you do for us?"

I told him briefly, just touching on our earlier success with the play.

"How much money you want?"

I named a figure and kind-of tightened up inside.

"Okay, he said," standing and offering his hand. "We'll think about that and be in touch."

Outside, I did not know what to make of that. Was it the world's shortest job interview or a quick brush-off? It felt a bit too abrupt, but then again, I thought, maybe that's how they do it in West Texas. Taciturn talk, handshake, and that's it.

I left.

The next day, one of his lieutenants– the one who would be my boss– called me and offered me the job at the salary I had asked for and even asked me to start immediately. I was there that afternoon– my most amazing job-getting experience ever had borne fruit. The job would become the fulcrum of a full return to confidence and success in the way I earned a living and lived my life.

The angel was right.

PART SEVEN

The Path

CHAPTER TWENTY-FOUR

THE PROCESS OF RECOVERY MUST SPAN the rest of one's mortal life, but the return to full-functioning real-world effectiveness is what the doc and I had been talking about. That job at the TV station began that part of the process, the one leading to full social functioning. For me that was a ten- to twenty-year slog, but once the milestone was reached, the closet had been cleaned out, the detractors I met along the way dismissed, and productive balance in life restored.

Forever hanging overhead, though, was that sword, the sword of Damocles, the reality that continuous sobriety was necessary. One slip, one binge and all progress reverts to the starting point– if I could live through it. Many do not.

During the slog, the years of personal growth, my life improved in uneven increments. Self-worth returned, my spiritual side re-kindled. But many times it was two-steps forward, three-steps backwards. And the Mad Hatter– whom I thought I had sent out to play in the traffic– showed up a few more times, but only briefly. The urge to get in the Ferrari– to drink again– would come with stealth at times, too. But such times gradually lost their power. The literature and shared experiences tell us that those times will come. But something stands in the gap. It is what the book *Alcoholics Anonymous*, calls "our spiritual condition."

I've had that experience. Twice. It tells us that times will come when our spiritual condition is the only thing between us and a drink. The book is correct. It happens. And the experience lit my path with torches ensconced in gold .

The aphorism's truth was confirmed for me one day in Virginia Beach. I was there on business and had been running all day. Things were not going well. In fact, I was downright angry at some folks. At midday, I stopped at a resort hotel to make a phone call (again, the times were those Cro-Magnon days before cell phones). The surf and sun beckoned just yards away. There is nothing like the undulating rhythms of the Atlantic lapping the sand in a continuous echo of our planet's most ancient days. Seductive memories of years long since past beckoned.

But because these were formative times for me, my anger turned a deaf ear on the echoes of God's creation, and I went to the phone booth. All around me, a convention was in full toot. When I emerged from yet another angry telephone conversation, my eyes were drawn, like magnets, to the open bar just steps away. Jovial conventioneers bellied up. My rage began to dissipate.

Within seconds, the Mad Hatter was back, taunting me. I was in the midst of a thick, dark jungle– far from "the path that does not stray"– facing an angry black mamba, the fastest snake in the world. I reacted instantly... the wrong way.

My thinking slithered to a baleful conclusion: no one knows me here. Surely the only thing that could change my lousy attitude was a drink. I could have just one. It would help, like medicine, to void this bad day. I would return to Richmond, and no one would be the wiser.

In the very next instant, the acronym HALT popped into my mind. It was something I had learned over my then ten-years of sobriety: *avoid becoming Hungry, Angry, Lonely, or Tired*. The condition can lead to a drink.

I heard that, surely God's message. I turned and hastened to the hotel's general restaurant where I ate a fifteen-dollar lunch...with iced tea, unsweetened.

Next, I called a friend, one with many years of experience with recovery and wise beyond his years.

"So...what're you going to do now," he said, after I told him what had just happened.

"I'm going back to Richmond, find a discussion group, and throw my experience on the floor for discussion."

"Damn right you are," he said. "And if you don't, I'm coming after you, and a couple of us ex-Marines will haul your butt to the gooney roost. You will call me after the meeting." Click.

"There will come a time when the only thing between you and a drink will be your spiritual condition:" words that very conceivably could have saved my life that day, and would stay with me as companion on the Path.

The inlet at the north end of Wrightsville Beach, North Carolina marks the meeting of the Atlantic and the inland waterway that makes its course betwixt the marinas, condos, tourist haunts, and hotels running along the western periphery of the resort area.

Spits of sand form the opening. Near nightfall, my son and I stood on the tip of the southern jetty. Peaceful it was not. Under angry, roiling gray clouds, the Atlantic assaulted the land barrier, winds howling, surf foaming. A northeaster was about to make landfall. A Christmas northeaster.

Awestruck by nature's power, we stood as the gale grew and wailed, while surf-foam became airborne. I reflected, as the onslaught's sheer presence forced clarity of mind. There was nothing to do but stand there and experience the sea's power and majesty. Nothing else needed to be done. The sea carried its own message.

We dallied for a long time, reluctant to go back to the family's annual holiday gathering in Wilmington. We had hiked out to that point over perhaps a quarter of a mile of sand's expanse to the storm's attack on the inlet. Taking a break from family dynamics was welcome, for some of my memories still carried old baggage. I was in my second decade of sobriety, "profound personality change" in full bloom. But it was okay, for there was unstated understanding of where I was. We are a resilient clan.

The gale squalled and the white-topped waves serially slapped into each other as they broke violently on the sand barrier. Nature is a great therapist.

It has been a much longer time now. Looking back, I wonder what's different. Life's become pretty normal. Many may be puzzled by what "normal" is, but I know, because I have a baseline. Normal is not losing the way of "the path that does not stray"– poetry describing a path which if lost leads to a completely dystopian disconnect from sane living.

Normal is pretty much working Monday through Friday. Going now to a second generation of youth baseball games to watch my offspring's offspring compete. Keeping up a house. Participating in my church. Normal is seeing my two children– perhaps my best friends today– now grown and succeeding in their lives. And it is five grandchildren who never saw their "Poppy" drunk.

It took losing my way in order to find it, which I did only by the grace of God. And God let that happen so that I could tell this story– a story that I pray will help others avoid the same mistakes I made all those years ago.

The sun is setting now, casting a red celestial curtain across the forested horizon before me. Life moves on. Creation's counsel is dramatic but subtle. Silence alone inspires. And again I ask, where does this "normal" lead?

My story shows the way– through just as many paths as there are people with chemical dependency problems. All paths, however, will run parallel. Some will finally meld into one– "The Path," the one which follows the basic principles of recovery.

Take care, I must, for the path is not through some kind of monastic solipsism. Isolation is the bane of recovery, dangerous turf for many. The way is through the comradery of one alcoholic or drug addict with another– connections that work but are hard to explain, but I try. My experience, and that of the millions throughout the world who have found the miracle of recovery, supports that belief, that process.

First, beware– for the enemies of recovery are legion:

ENABLERS: "Keep your friends close," goes a popular saying, "and your enemies even closer." Wise advice, but distorted when it comes to "enablers." They are people, usually relatives or close friends, who "enable" alcohol or other drug abuse to continue unchallenged. They do so unwittingly, just thinking of themselves as friends. So the friends-and-enemies formula reverses. Enabling friends can become enemies by endorsing victimology and thus prolong dysfunctional behavior, especially chemical dependency.

PEER PRESSURE: Friends should not let friends get hooked, but they do. And the abuser is driven by a need to be accepted, to fit in, to be one of the group. A deadly symbiosis sets in.

CULTURE: Contemporary music, media, and mores can all effectively endorse addictive behavior. The classic motion picture *Casablanca*, forever a favorite of mine, always comes to mind when I think about this.

The suave "Rick," Humphrey Bogart's award-winning character, is never without a cigarette... or a drink. As time goes by, the lithe and lovely Ingrid Bergman as Ilsa comes on the scene and is ever around (until her plane comes in, anyway)... enabling. The message I got was that smoking and drinking were "cool," so if I wanted to be too, I should do both. I did.

The need to be accepted, and with a ticket to the party, eerily but accurately echoes something my mother told me over and over: "Never go along with the crowd just to make others think highly of you or without thinking it through." I had forgotten that at the worst possible time in my life.

For these and other reasons, my experience– and those of many others– I believe must be heard. Otherwise, those stories are like blades of grass in a great field, or barely perceptible ripples on the face of an endless sea. They must be told before the constant winds carry them away. We who've walked the walk share our experiences, our strengths, our failings, and our hopes for the future with those who will be helped by them... and those who want to be.

Some will find my words laughable– a foolish, needless self-exposure– for many walk around encased in walls of guilt. But it will always come out sideways when most unwelcome.

Some it will insult, like the guy in my former church. Some cannot entertain the truth. We are fallible beings who tell ourselves we couldn't be fallible beings.

Others will take it as a cultural abomination to spill personal secrets– those things that should be kept within families, they will say– but their fallacy is that many families are also encased in guilt: guilt that stands a good chance of one day seeing the light of day in a way that will not shower honorifics on that family.

"But what about your family?" they will say.

Well, it's contagious. The family's got it, too– at least the "-ism" anyway. Remember: "alcoholism is a family disease."

A few of us will come to defy the lies– lies that dance around the truth. Some of us may even have to turn our backs on enabling families and friends, to seek recovery and thus respite from the drooling living death alcoholism and other chemical dependencies can bring.

It is to those few– the seekers– that I write. May God bless and protect them, whoever and wherever they are and whenever their light appears.

It had started on "the worst day of my life" with my mind's eye on that ominous image of the Luger in the drawer where it had lain, awaiting a loaded magazine, for most of my remembrance.

It would end, years later after my folks had passed on, when once again I went to get the Luger. By then, more than a quarter of a century had passed since my crisis, and the weapon was back in its place.

I took the Luger to the indoor shooting range where I had taught my son and two grandsons gun safety, but this time I was by myself with something to prove, and a demon to assassinate.

I began my routine firing nine-millimeter rounds in groups of threes at standard targets. I reeled the targets in and checked my accuracy and just kept doing that, over and over, spacing the targets at varying distances from my position on the firing line. The range was busy. More than half of the shooters were women, I noticed. Surely a sign of the times. One I welcomed.

The sounds were continuous— everything from twenty-two-caliber target pistols to forty-five- and fifty-caliber guns of all types: pistols, revolvers, rifles and war-like semi-automatic weapons, including that day someone with a Thompson submachine gun. Like scenes from an old Elliott Ness movie, black-and-white images of Chicago gang-wars of the roaring 20s flickered in my mind.

Ear- and eye-protection was mandatory. Managers oversaw the firing through sound-deadening double-paned protective windows all along the firing line.

Cordite smells hung in the air. A cacophony of brass chimed as streams of spent cartridges hit the polished concrete floor. I conjured a warzone, knowing it my own.

Close to obsessed, I was totally focused on the accuracy of my endless series of three-round patterns on the cardboard targets. The idea was to place each group of three within a circle about the diameter of a quarter. I had always been pretty good at it.

I have no idea how long it took to shoot up the four boxes of fifty rounds each. But by the time I finished, my shot-groups were better than ninety-percent perfect at any distance I chose. I was zoned.

Being zoned was a natural high. I first experienced it in my tennis-playing days, and later when I joined the running craze of the 70s and 80s. The zone's euphoria would sometimes last into the following day. And the experience, as I learned then, can herald a life-changing time. So it was for me that day on the range.

After I finished, I cleared and cleaned the Luger, packed up and left. Something moved in my soul. I walked lighter on the path to my car. And I knew why.

The following night I had agreed to meet a man in the darkened parking lot of one of West End Richmond's shopping centers. It was mostly empty that late. I pulled up beside the large, black SUV the man was driving. We had been talking about this for a while, for he was a collector of World War II weapons. And I was selling the Luger to him.

He examined the fateful weapon whose story he knew not, and we made a deal, as I knew we would. I left. On my way home, I felt a burden flee, leaving behind a significant symbol of times past.

Yes, I was a War Baby. And in that last obsessive shooting session, with that proud weapon from the war of the Greatest Generation, I felt the fears and tensions of my war leave me just as dramatically as they had begun. The hedgerows among paths both dark and light withered, leaving me on new ground.

My war was over.

ENDNOTES AND COMMENTS

[1] Dr. J.B. Rhine and others founded the Parapsychology Laboratory of Duke University in 1930. It became a separate entity in 1965: The Institute of Parapsychology under the sponsorship of the Foundation for Research on the Nature of Man.

[2] Zener Cards attracted considerable skepticism, which was addressed by Dr. Rhine in his book, *Extra-Sensory Perception*, first published in 1962 and now available in paperback, published by Brandon Publishing Company, Boston.

[3] From *Alice's Adventures in Wonderland* by Lewis Carroll. Carroll did not call the Hatter "mad," but the Cheshire Cat did, to Alice: "In that direction," the Cat said, "lives a Hatter: and in that direction, lives a March Hare. Visit either you like. They're both mad."

[4] Williams, Tennessee (1983). *Cat on a Hot Tin Roof*. New York: Signet.

[5] The Richmond Times-Dispatch, Richmond, Virginia, pages 1 and 9, March 8, 1946, and pages 1 and 5, March 9, 1946.

[6] A variety of records held in the Library of The Virginia Historical Society, Richmond. In 1940, after the last Veteran who had lived there died, Robinson House became State property and headquarters of Robert E. Lee Camp Number 1 of Confederate Veterans. Confederate veterans continued to live in nearby barracks, since torn down, and in the Richmond area. They continued to gather regularly in the park around the Robinson House. The last Veteran to have lived in Richmond was George Bannister, who died in 1949 at the age of 100, following a successful peacetime career as a bartender and restaurateur.

7   The Virginia Museum Theater was founded in 1955 as a part of the Virginia Museum of Fine Arts in Richmond. It flourished as a community theater with professional leadership well into the 1970s when it was replaced by TheatreVirginia, a professional equity theater, which closed in 2002, following financial and administrative problems.

8   Troop 660 was originally Troop 60, Robert E. Lee Council, BSA. It later became Troop 760 after the Lee Council was renamed Heart of Virginia Council, BSA. It has been hosted continuously by Lakeside Presbyterian Church, Henrico, Virginia, for nearly 80 years.

9   Goodwin, Donald W., *Alcoholism: The Facts*, (New York, Oxford University Press, Inc., Third Edition, 2000) 18 through 21.

10 Dr. Benjamin Rush's views are referenced by Levine, Harry G., "The Discovery of Addiction: Changing Conceptions of Habitual Drunkenness in America" *Journal of Studies on Alcohol.* 1978; 15: pp. 493-506. Dr. Rush's original work on the subject is *Inquiry into the Effects of Ardent Spirits upon the Human Body and Mind.* (Philadelphia, Bartam, 1805).

11 *Diagnostic and Statistical Manual of Mental Disorders*, Fourth Edition, Text Revision. (Washington, D.C., American Psychiatric Association, 2000) Page 197.

12 "Abraham Lincoln on Alcoholism," Address to the Washington Temperance Society, February 22, 1842, reprinted in *The A.A. Grapevine*, February 1964, Alcoholics Anonymous World Services, Inc., New York.

13 The Landmark Theater has undergone extensive improvements and was renamed Altria Theater early in 2014.

14 Jellinek, E.M., *The Disease Concept of Alcoholism*, 1960 (Reprinted as a paperback in 2010 by Martino Fine Books, Eastford, Connecticut).

15 My "test" was perhaps the shortest of a number that health care practitioners use. It is called the CAGE test and is meant to be a quick assessment: 1. Have you ever tried to Cut down on your drinking? 2. Do you get Angry when people discuss your drinking? 3. Do you feel Guilty about things you may have done while drinking? 4. Do you ever have an Eye-opener (that is, do you ever take a drink to get rid of a hangover of the start the day)? This test, the widely used Michigan Alcoholism Screening Test (MAST), and others are discussed in *Beyond the Influence* by Katherine Ketchum and William F. Asbury (New York, Bantam Books, 2000) Pages 112 and following.

[16] Now in his 80s, Van Dyke is something of a legend in recovery circles. He has maintained sobriety and freely shares his story in a recent memoir, *My Lucky Life, In and Out of Show Business*, (New York, Crown, 2011).

[17] Wilbur Mills' Tidal Basin episode was Page 1 news in *The Washington Post*, October 11, 1974. The story was written by Stephen Green and Margot Hornblower with eight other Post staffers contributing.

[18] Albert Einstein. BrainyQuote.com, Xplore Inc, 2012. http://www.brainyquote.com/quotes/quotes/a/alberteins130891.html, accessed September 7, 2012.

[19] "Positive addictions" for me would include over the ensuing years, the running phase of the late 70s and 80s. I was running several days a week as much as 10 miles at a time. That was followed, prompted by the hint of beginnings of knee problems in my early 40s, by my swimming phase. Next came a return to my first sports love, tennis. I did that as often as possible. And as age crept up, I settled in to a general walking and strength-training jag, that continues to this day.

[20] *Vitae Summa Brevis Spem Nos Vetat Incohare Longam*, a 19th Century poem by Ernest Dowson. BrainyQuote.com, Xplore Inc., 2012. http://www.brainyquote.com/quotes/quotes/e/ernestdows368467.html.

[21] Wilson, Bill, *As Bill Sees It* (New York, Alcoholics Anonymous World Services, First Edition, 1967).

[22] Didion, Joan, *The Year of Magical Thinking*, (New York, Vintage Books, First Vintage International Edition, 2007) 22.

[23] *Ibid*. 33.

[24] Dufty, William, *Sugar Blues*, (New York, Warner Books, 1975). *Sugar Blues* is a very convincing book on the health dangers of refined white sugar. Immediately, I stopped adding sugar to the many cups of coffee I would down in a day. Tasted bad at first, but it's all in what you get used to, so in a way tangential to alcoholism.

[25] *Alcoholics Anonymous*, (New York, Alcoholics Anonymous World Services, Inc., Fourth Edition, 2001) 59-60. The Twelve Steps of Alcoholics Anonymous:
   1. We admitted we were powerless over alcohol– that our lives had become unmanageable.
   2. Came to believe that a Power greater than ourselves could restore us to sanity.

3. Made a decision to turn our will and our lives over to the care of God *as we understood Him.*

4. Made a searching and fearless moral inventory of ourselves.

5. Admitted to God, to ourselves, and to another human being the exact nature of our wrongs.

6. Were entirely ready to have God remove all these defects of character.

7. Humbly asked Him to remove our shortcomings.

8. Made a list of all persons we had harmed, and became willing to make amends to them all.

9. Made direct amends to such people wherever possible, except when to do so would injure them or others.

10. Continued to take personal inventory, and when we were wrong, promptly admitted it.

11. Sought through prayer and meditation to improve our conscious contact with God *as we understood Him,* praying only for knowledge of His will for us and the power to carry that out.

12. Having had a spiritual awakening as the result of these steps, we tried to carry this message to alcoholics, and to practice these principles in all our affairs.

26 Hoff, Ebbe Curtis, MD, *Alcoholism: The Hidden Addiction,* (New York, The Seabury Press, 1974). Biographical summary: Dr. Hoff was a native of Rexford, Kansas, graduate of the University of Washington; doctor of philosophy, St. Catherine's College, Oxford; bachelor's degree in medicine and surgery and doctorate in medicine, plus master of surgery from both Oxford and the London Hospital and Medical College. He taught physiology and worked as a research assistant at Yale University. In the Navy he became an authority on submarine and aviation medicine and served on the team that developed an improved "G-suit" for Naval aviators. He left the active navy with the rank of Commander but continued his service in the U.S. Navy Reserve. He was also an amateur radio operator, WA4CBM.

27 Ibid., Foreword by Dr. Sexias.

ACKNOWLEDGEMENTS

First things first: Thanks to the Rev. J. David Singh, a longtime friend, counselor, and pastor, for providing the original encouragement to write *War Baby*. Joshua Paul Cane, Fred Larmore and David Singh became a sort-of rolling writing critique group, much to my benefit. Raymond Wallace offered incisive commentary and support along the way. My enduring thanks to Gigi Amateau, Dean King, David Robbins, and Logan Ward– all experts in their field– for their shared experiences and inspiration. Logan, in particular, spent valuable time early on, prompting me to write "scenically... cinematically–" stuff that can elude old journalists in a gnat's blink. To my wonderful children, writer-daughter Elizabeth Blue Wheeler and son "DB4," thank you for leading cheers during this journey. Thank you, also, to my kindred pal–Lucy Alfriend Thacker– who made it her mission to design this book through my mind's eye. And to the membership, board and supporters of James River Writers: I must say, without you all– this undertaking would have been so much more daunting. Special thanks to the Virginia Historical Society, the Library of Virginia, the Valentine Richmond History Center, the Henrico County, Virginia Libraries... and for unfailing jump-starts of my creative engine, the Virginia Museum of Fine Arts. Finally– last, but also first– I have been most richly blessed by the many friendships among "the recovery community," their counselors and healthcare providers. They are all miracles, heroines, and heroes, dwelling, working, and laughing among us... while we may not even know it.

–Doug Blue
Ashland, Virginia

ABOUT THE AUTHOR

Dougald L. "Doug" Blue III started writing when he was about eight with a biography about Alexander the Great– researched and borderline-plagiarized from *National Geographic* magazine and a book his dad gave him. At twelve, he wrote, set type and printed his own neighborhood newspaper, making a killing at five cents a copy. His adult career began as a copyboy, intern, and city-desk reporter for the *Richmond Times-Dispatch* during the golden years of newspapers. That was followed by some 35 years in corporate communications, and then the inevitable "self-employment," now working as a writer, editor, and publicist. He is an alumnus of Hampden-Sydney College where good writing is a valued achievement, as well as a necessity. A native of Richmond, he resides today in nearby Ashland, Virginia. Contact him through his website– http://dougaldblue.com or via email– boblue3@comcast.net.

Made in the USA
Charleston, SC
06 November 2014